Drug and Alcohol Depen...

DRUG and ALCOHOL DEPENDENCY NURSING

JAMES KENNEDY SRN, RMN, DipNursing
Assistant Unit General Manager, Priority Services Unit,
Islington Health Authority

and

JEAN FAUGIER RMN, RCNT, DipNursing,
DANS, RNT, MSc, DipPsychotherapy
Lecturer, Manchester Polytechnic

HEINEMANN NURSING

Heinemann Nursing
An imprint of Heinemann Professional Publishing Ltd
Halley Court, Jordan Hill, Oxford OX2 8EJ

OXFORD LONDON SINGAPORE NAIROBI
IBADAN KINGSTON

First published 1989

© James Kennedy and Jean Faugier 1989

British Library Cataloguing in Publication Data
Kennedy, J.
    Drug and alcohol dependency nursing.
    1.   Alcoholism & drug addiction. Therapy
    I.   Title   II.   Faugier, J.
    616.86

ISBN 0 433 00016 3

Typeset by R. H. Services, Welwyn, Hertfordshire
Printed and bound in Great Britain by Biddles Ltd, Guildford

Contents

Acknowledgements

It is impossible to thank individually all those clients, colleagues and friends who have enabled us to complete the writing of this book. However, we are particularly indebted to those clients and colleagues whom we have encountered during our work at the Alcohol ꞏ roblem Advisory Service in Bloomsbury, London (especially Seonaid Wright for the advice on page 84) and the Department of Nursing at Manchester Polytechnic; also to the students who have completed the ENB Course 612 in London and Manchester and who provided us with useful stimulation. Specific thanks are due to Christine Burke and Lyn Meehan, who completed the typing of the manuscript.

We are also grateful to members of the Association of Nurses in Substance Abuse, who often provided us with a forum for discussion and debate about many of the issues which have been outlined in this book. Finally, the support of our partners, Gillian and Regis, enabled the job to be eventually finished.

James Kennedy
Jean Faugier

Foreword

In virtually all of the countries of the world huge demands are placed upon health and social services by the adverse consequences of psychoactive drugs. These substances, alcohol, tobacco, prescribed and illicit drugs, are very widely used and this popularity engenders a massive and tragic toll of dependence, accidents, morbidity and mortality. In spite of the importance of drug-related health damage very few health professionals receive much, if any, formal training to prepare them to cope with such problems.

Available evidence indicates that, for many of those with alcohol or other drug-related problems the prognosis is surprisingly good. Such problems are far from being intractable. Many of those who drink or use other drugs with adverse consequences to themselves or to others do overcome or reduce their difficulties. A variety of therapeutic and counselling approaches exist which can help and support the 'problem drinker' or the 'problem drug user'. Many of these approaches have value and no single method appears to be uniquely successful. Similarly, no single professional group has been shown to outshine others in the provision of health care or other support for those with alcohol and drug problems. The latter require a multidisciplinary response which often necessitates good health care as well as counselling and a 'user friendly' approach. Nurses are a very important part of the response to alcohol and other drug problems. A considerable proportion of nursing time is devoted to those who suffer directly or indirectly from such problems. These include the victims of drunken drivers, the spouses or children of problem drinkers, people who are dependent upon benzodiazepines, alcohol, tobacco or illicit drugs. Drug problems have assumed an even more ominous nature since the advent of the AIDS pandemic. In many areas the major method by which HIV infection is being transmitted is through intravenous drug use. In addition, growing evidence suggests that people are much more likely to become exposed to such infection when under the disinhibiting effects of substances such as alcohol, cannabis or cocaine.

In this excellent volume James Kennedy and Jean Faugier bring together a valuable array of information and experience. The chapters on nursing interventions in this book acknowledge the diversity of therapeutic approaches and should help to erode the mystique of working with people who are in some way damaged by the excessive or inappropriate use of psychoactive drugs.

Moira Plant RGN RMN PhD
Alcohol Research Group
University of Edinburgh

Introduction

The 1980s have seen a great increase in the number of people using and abusing both legal and illegal substances. For most of us, this period has been one of enormous social change, bringing with it positive and negative developments which have a direct effect on people's lives. Some of these changes are widely viewed by society as beneficial, for example the changing role of women, some of whom now have more personal freedom than previously was the case. Other changes such as unemployment and regional economic decline, are seen as damaging the very fabric of society itself.

No matter how one views the enormous changes that have taken place over the last three decades, they have certainly brought great pressures to bear on individuals and families. These pressures, whether they stem from objective external factors such as the loss of a job and subsequent lack of money, or from subjective internal stresses such as unrealistic expectations, often result in people seeking relief by the use of drugs. This is not new; drugs have been used, legally or illegally, for a long time to deal with either real or perceived 'pain', and to escape for a while from the unpleasant reality of a difficult situation. Nor is there anything novel about dependence on drugs, which constitutes one of the most important problems of modern society. Over the centuries, there is scarcely any mood-altering substance that has not been used and abused simultaneously in one society or another.

The varying level of popularity of different drugs has historically depended on such influences as fashion, economics and simple availability. The 'drug of choice' in Western society – recently referred to as 'our favourite drug' by the Royal College of Psychiatrists (1986) – is alcohol. Alcohol is legally available in all Western industrialised nations. It plays an important part in life for most of us, and contributes to the economic structure of society by the creation of jobs and the revenue from taxation. Virtually all major events in our culture are marked by the use of alcohol; social gatherings within the family or wider society for the purpose of celebration or commiseration are

1

frequently, if not always, 'lubricated' by the use of beverage alcohol. This development, as Gossop (1982) explains, was in some ways forced upon European society by the lack of choice of indigenous drugs: Europe had no tea, coffee or tobacco, and only small quantities of opium or hallucinatory drugs. However, it *did* have a climate and soil ideal for the production of various forms of alcohol. Alcohol remains the preferred, legal and socially acceptable drug throughout Europe, and as yet no other substance has managed to become a comparable part of our social existence. It is an increasingly popular drug, and is so linked with every aspect of our lives that we tend to deny the bad effects it can have.

Society seems to suffer from a similarly irrational attitude to the use of other mind-altering drugs. Whilst effectively condoning the massive and increasing use of prescribed drugs, in particular psychotropic ones such as the benzodiazepines, society throws its hands up in horror at the increasing use of illegal substances such as heroin and cocaine. Witness to this societal ambivalence is the concentration of the media and government education campaigns on the misuse of illegal substances, whereas the misuse of prescribed drugs and the problems they incur elicit much less response. There are many reasons why this is so, the main one being the legal nature of alcohol and prescribed drugs, as well as the fact that they form part of our normative experience.

Illegal drugs such as heroin, cocaine and amphetamines are for most of us outside our normal experience, and being illegal, are seen as deviant, dangerous and morally wrong. However, the changing nature of society has made these drugs widely available to an increasing number of people, particularly the young, and drugs are now to some extent part of young people's normal experience through being a constant feature of the society in which they live. This increase in the number of people who use both illegal and legal drugs means that a greater proportion will find themselves, for different reasons, in trouble with regard to their drug use. This 'trouble' can manifest itself in various ways, either physically, psychologically or socially, or a combination of all three.

The World Health Organisation clearly recognises the interaction of both physical and psychological processes in their 1969 definition of drug dependency:

'a state, psychic and sometimes also physical, resulting from the interaction between a living organism and a drug characterised by behavioural and other responses that always include a compulsion to take the drug on a continuous or periodic basis in order to experience its psychic effects, and sometimes to avoid the discomfort of its absence. Tolerance may or may not be present. A person may be dependent on more than one drug.'

This definition also recognises an increasingly alarming development in people who abuse various substances: 'polydrug' abuse. Increasingly, those who have a problem with drink may also abuse drugs, and recently observed evidence suggests that many young drug abusers involved in the use of heroin or cannabis will drink heavily as well. As Hofman (1983) states:

'the widely held belief that drug and alcohol abuse are fundamentally different is misleading, they are not.'

Society may display quite different attitudes towards drinking and drug usage and react as though the two are significantly dissimilar, but the fact remains that the salient features of drug and alcohol misuse are almost identical.

It is with this in mind that we discuss dependence and abuse from a 'continuum' perspective. This continuum of drug-taking experience and dependence-producing behaviour should not be seen as something related to a small minority of people with problems, but as part of everyone's experience and a potential problem for all of us. It is essential, therefore, that nurses working in this field of study start by examining their own attitudes to drugs and dependence, and perhaps explode a number of myths and stereotypes in respect of drug and alcohol abuse.

REFERENCES

Gossop M. (1982). *Living with Drugs*. London: Temple Smith.

Hofman F. G. (1983). *A Handbook on Drug and Alcohol Abuse – The Biomedical Aspects*. Oxford: OUP.

Royal College of Psychiatrists (1986). *Alcohol: our favourite drug*. London: Tavistock.

Chapter 1

The nature of dependency

Historical perspective

For our purposes in this book, a drug is defined as any chemical that alters mood. We include alcohol as a drug – in fact a drug on which our society is dependent, not simply for its mood-changing properties but in all manner of social and economic ways.

Historically, most societies (if not all) have used mind-altering drugs. Theories of how the properties of these substances were discovered can only be speculative, but it seems reasonable to imagine that early humans stumbled by accident on the production of alcohol by plant and cereal fermentation, and the effects of eating or sucking certain types of plant, roots or other vegetation. The scenario usually presented is that our early ancestors, in the course of their hunting expeditions, or perhaps lost in the woods or mountains, would, in an attempt to stave off hunger and cold, resort to eating whatever they could find. Perhaps they would also light a fire made of branches or plants found by chance. They then found that some of these plants or roots, when eaten or inhaled via the fumes from the fire, produced a pleasant effect, often a change in consciousness and a hallucinatory experience; thus, the use of such substances became incorporated into the culture of early civilisations. According to Glatt and Marks (1982), these hallucinatory experiences could easily be explained as the voices and visions of the various gods to which a particular civilisation adhered. The advent of ritual in the use of mind-altering substances was an effective way for early civilisations to control abuse. Glatt and Marks (1982) stated that: 'almost without exception, the ritual use of psychotropic substances precludes their abuse'. Examples of ritualistic control of psychotropic substances are the controlled use of opium smoking in Eastern religions, alcohol controls in orthodox Jewish communities, the use of coca leaf by early Inca civilisation and the use of mescaline by the Native American Church of North America. Gossop (1982) argues that the early ritualisation of alcohol into Christian society, and the revulsion

5

held for other mind-altering drugs by the church, had as much to do with alcohol achieving its dominance in European nations as did the relative absence of other drugs. Prior to the voyages of discovery, to the Americas in particular, which introduced into our culture tobacco and cocaine, other substances including hallucinogenic mushrooms and cannabis were available to Europeans, who apparently chose not to use these substances in any significant numbers.

Society is now responding in an alarmed fashion to heroin and cocaine as if it had no previous historical experience of these substances. Heroin was in fact discovered in 1874 by a London chemist, C. R. Alder-Wright. This discovery was made some seventy years after morphine had been isolated from opium. The substance was given the name heroin by Heinrich Dresser in 1898. Chief pharmacologist for the Frederick Bayer company in Germany, Dresser reported that his tests in the laboratory on animals and limited human trials led him to believe that the new product was a very good treatment for all forms of respiratory disease, including tuberculosis and bronchitis. Thus, the first contribution made by heroin to society was in the form of a cough medicine which, its creator argued, had no unpleasant side effects – as opposed to morphine, which often had. Judson (1973) cites the now almost incredible fact that, when listing heroin's heroic properties, Dresser mentioned that the drug seemed not to be habit forming!

The pleasures of opium use and its potential to produce dependence have long been known throughout the world, and Europeans were using opium for the relief of pain and the seeking of pleasure long before the discovery of heroin. The most famous European opium users include some of the best-known names in English literature: Byron, Keats, Shelley, Coleridge and De Quincey all regularly used opium. In the later 'bohemian' movements of the 1960s, the use of illegal drugs was often linked to the belief that they would unleash creative potential. However, as Hofman (1983) points out, the English author De Quincey was under no illusions about any creative ability brought on by the drug, and did not believe that use of the drug could produce previously non-existent patterns of thought or behaviour. De Quincey argued that if one had not dreamed beautiful dreams before taking opium, one would not do so under its influence.

Gossop (1982) points out that the use of opium in England was not confined to poets and writers; it was used in various forms as a folk remedy for such conditions as malaria, which was endemic at the time in East Anglia. In many cases, opium was used in preference to alcohol, and the use of laudanum – a combination of alcohol and tincture of opium – was historically common in England, particularly among the poor. Certainly, in the mid-nineteenth century, opium use was seen as quite normal, often beneficial, and certainly not a cause for social concern.

The history of alcohol use stems from the most primitive times. Mentions of alcohol and alcohol consumption are present in the Bible. Even the tombs of ancient Egyptians display evidence on their walls of the methods of alcohol production. The ancient Greeks had a god of wine, Dionysus, who was able through the use of wine to help the soul to transcend the body. The Romans, according to history, displayed less control in their attitude to drinking, especially in the later periods of the Roman Empire, and alcohol use in vast amounts, often associated with other activities of a hedonistic or sexual nature, became common at Roman banquets.

A turning point in the history of alcohol came with the discovery of distillation and the production of spirits. This meant that greater effect could be produced by drinking less liquid in quantity. Distilled alcohol is thought to have been first described by Jabir ibn Hayijan (712–813 AD) in an Arabic manuscript, but due to its forbidden status in Moslem society, was apparently forgotten until rediscovered by Lully (1235–1315 AD), a Franciscan monk in southern France. This time the climate was right for the new substance to become very popular, and, as Glatt and Marks (1982) point out, the practice of distillation spread rapidly throughout Europe, producing changes in consciousness, often in the form of acute and chronic drunkenness. Shaw *et al.* (1978) claim that widespread drunkenness was documented as early as the mid-seventeenth century, and that taverns and inns serving cheap distilled alcohol as well as beer and wines became favourite meeting places for criminals and people of ill repute (this, among other historical factors, accounts for alcohol's long association with the production of criminal behaviour). By the mid-eighteenth century, the drinking of very cheap gin had reached epidemic proportions. Every town and city had numerous gin houses which, as Gossop (1982) indicates, provided lessons to the advertising media of today by displaying signs claiming that clients could become drunk for a penny and dead drunk for twopence. In those days, advertising standards were a little less evident . . .

Alcohol and other drugs thus have long and colourful histories, and their relationship with various societies and cultures has shaped our ambivalent attitudes towards them. This history is by no means completed, and the current worldwide developments in alcohol and drug use are changing once more the manner in which these substances are viewed. Medical knowledge, an increase in health consciousness and an alarm at the spread of dependence means that increased efforts are now being made by various groups of professionals to understand how historical developments have coloured our perception of alcohol and drug misuse, and consequently our approaches to treating the problems they produce for individuals, families and society in general.

Changing patterns and current developments

Drug users fall into a number of not very clearly defined nor exclusive groups or categories. Current thinking in the substance abuse field tends towards the belief that, whilst society's attitudes towards certain substances may differ, the underlying mechanisms involved in the production of dependency are in many ways very similar.

Glatt and Marks (1982) suggested that we operate on a hierarchical principle of abused substances, beginning with those that most of us use and would accept socially, such as tea, coffee, tobacco, beer, wine and spirits. A large group of people within most industrialised societies indulges in the use and perhaps the abuse of those substances. A smaller group of people uses – and again perhaps abuses – prescribed drugs (either self or medically prescribed). Whilst society recognises that this is a problem for some of those individuals, the drugs tend not to be seen as 'bad' drugs and the people involved are not generally seen as deviant. An even smaller group of people will be using and abusing substances that are deemed illegal, such as heroin, cannabis, cocaine or LSD. These people are seen as very different from the other, larger, groups in society involved in drug use of all kinds. One of the reasons for this is the stigma attached to the subcultural criminal scene in which illegal drug users are forced to operate. But as Scheff (1967) points out, a deviant label is rapidly attached to anyone in our society who is involved in breaking the residual rules of our social culture.

Recently, the numbers of drug users of all types have increased, and dependence on drugs is looked upon as one of the biggest threats to the way of life in Western society. Currently, with the possible exception of concern about AIDS (which is also linked to drug abuse), it takes precedence in terms of political initiatives, and governments of many nations are involved in campaigns or legislation attempting to control drug abuse of various types. In the West, alarm has most recently been aroused by the growing use of illegal drugs, although there is increased concern also about the rapid rise in problem drinking. In the Eastern bloc countries, a major concern is the widespread and alarming rise in problem drinking. In Britain, a major set of initiatives, including the setting up of three courses to train specialist nurses (ENB 612), followed publication of the Advisory Council's report, *Treatment and Rehabilitation* (DHSS 1982). This report and one on prevention published the following year (DHSS 1983) were made in response to the increasing alarm at the misuse of drugs generally, but in particular of illegal substances among young people. The first report (DHSS 1982) states:

> 'The misuse of drugs in the United Kingdom has increased substantially in the last few years but it remains confined to a relatively small percentage of the population. However, the

consequences for that small but increasing percentage are serious and may prevent individuals from functioning as effective members of society.'

These comments from a body with the influence of the Advisory Council are very significant, in that they present a somewhat narrow view of what constitutes drug misuse. The report further states:

'It is therefore essential to make a thorough and critical examination of the way in which society responds to drug misuse.'

Certainly we would agree that if we are to understand why some people have problems with illegal drugs, then it is essential to undertake a thorough and critical examination of the way we often view such problems as separate and different from those encountered by larger groups of people with socially accepted drugs such as alcohol and prescribed drugs.

In the majority of countries, the problems posed by socially acceptable drugs such as alcohol and the overprescribing of tranquillisers are much greater than those posed by illegal drugs. However, it would be wrong to suggest that there have not been great changes as far as illegal drugs are concerned; indeed, their use by ever-wider sections of American youth has led to a change of attitudes, in that it is now regarded as a less deviant, more normative behaviour by the general public; a similar pattern is also emerging in Britain. In 1979 over 5 million people in the USA had tried marijuana (cannabis) at least once in their lifetime, according to Relman (1982). It is clear from the literature that the use of marijuana has become a normative behaviour for much of American youth. Interestingly, Alterman (1985) points out that the use of the drug seems to have effectively crossed racial and class barriers, with very similar rates for young blacks and whites. Fishburne *et al.* (1980) also found that use of other drugs such as LSD, often seen as dangerous, was widespread, with 25% of young adults aged between 18 and 25 having used the drug at least once in their lifetime. Cocaine, a currently very popular stimulant drug, was similarly shown to be fairly widely used by college students in the USA.

Whilst these rates might seem alarming, Fishburne *et al.* (1980) found that approximately 60% of drug users take the drug fewer than ten times. This finding calls into question the previously held theories of drug misuse, often centred on the 'substance theory' which postulated that there was something immediately and inherently addictive about certain substances which would make controlled use or abstinence very difficult, if not impossible. Another interesting development, especially relating to heroin use, is the increase in 'smoking' as a means of using the drug. This smoking or inhaling ('chasing the dragon') is seen by many young people – quite legitimately – as much less dangerous or deviant than injecting the drug, and so brings use of the drug within the consideration of a wider group of people.

Concepts of dependence and addiction

Until recently, it was common for drug and alcohol dependence to be viewed firmly within the confines of the medical model of psychiatric care, as shown by Faugier (1986). This conventional concept of dependence owed much to the idea that some mysterious biological process (not yet identified) within the individual, or some special, almost magical, pharmaceutical properties of the particular substance, were powerful enough in themselves to account for the whole gamut of human behaviour we refer to as dependence. Both of these approaches have been plagued by massive contradictions, and both ideas, one placing responsibility for dependence on the substance, the other on the individual, were often used simultaneously and in relation to each other.

The substance theory

The 'substance theory' of dependence has dominated twentieth-century writing and thought in relation to narcotic drug addiction. The basis of the approach rests in the belief that the chemical properties of drugs (or families of drugs) will inevitably lead to the wide range of behaviour that we refer to as 'addiction' or 'dependence'. These exclusively biological explanations of dependency, whilst having lost much of their credibility, nevertheless exert strong and lasting influences on both professional and lay opinions about the nature of drugs.

Biological models of dependency unfortunately tend to foster a number of defeatist notions, many of which are used in a contradictory manner depending on the legality or otherwise of the substance under discussion, such as the 'one fix and you're hooked' exposure theory. This explanation is widely held by the general public, and also has a pervasive influence among professional workers. It suggests a frightening scenario in which a simple 'one-off' exposure to certain illegal narcotic substances will inevitably lead to addiction. Addiction or dependence is then viewed as being totally physiological, the body's need for the substance taking control and determining a whole range of social and psychological responses.

Tolerance, withdrawal symptoms and craving are thought to be the properties of particular drugs, and simple exposure with sufficient use of these substances is said to give the individual no choice (in a physiological sense) but to behave in these stereotypical ways (Peele 1985). This process is seen as being totally outside the person's control and, once the substance is used, the whole sequence of events is considered irreversible.

Illegal drugs are widely viewed in this manner as 'bad substances' which make the individual behave in an antisocial fashion, quite independently of social or psychological factors. In fact, the person under the influence of such dependence phenomena is often described as 'possessed', 'not themselves', a 'totally different person'. The implication is that the substance is all-powerful and does not leave the individual concerned any choice regarding its subsequent use. This process of physiologically produced dependence is thought to be essentially the same for human beings and animals, and the model clearly attempts to divorce human physiology from the individual's internal and external world.

The clearest contradiction in this theory comes in its application. Drugs such as heroin, cocaine and other narcotic analgesics are seen as universally addictive, with the locus of control in the substance and not in the individual. Health education campaigns continue to rely very heavily on this assumption, using fear arousal mechanisms intended to make young people fear the power of the drug to such an extent that they will avoid it at all costs.

For alcohol, however – an analgesic, depressive and sedative drug with many similar properties to the narcotics – the story needs to be changed. Since alcohol is the most universally available socially used drug, it would be inconceivable to have a theory of dependence that implicated the substance, as most of us have a strong and affectionate relationship with it. This being the case, we require a quite different explanation, and so it has become generally accepted that the fault with alcohol dependence lies not in the substance but in the individual. People who develop drinking problems are in some way different from the rest of society; they are suffering from the disease of alcoholism. The major similarities between the two explanations lie in the inevitability of the process and the issue of control. In the case of illegal drugs, the process of dependence is based on the power of the substance; but with legal drugs such as alcohol, the control lies in the power of the disease process.

The person/disease theory

The theory of dependence as a disease residing within the unfortunate individual is a concept rooted very deeply in the failure of prohibition movements and abstentionist organisations in relation to alcohol. The disastrous consequences of the experiment with prohibition were, as Laurie (1981) argues, more costly to American society than the problems produced by alcohol abuse. Indeed, in the period following the traumatic events of the prohibition period, people were not exactly open to an argument about alcoholic dependence and abuse that placed the blame on the substance and argued for its control. American society was therefore ready for any theory of alcohol dependence that would not advocate any wider societal response to the problem, particularly one that would restrict the availability of alcohol to the majority of the population who did not see it as a problem at all. The scene was set for the emergence of the most influential and well-developed self-help group of all time: Alcoholics Anonymous. An alliance between two problem drinkers, a New York stockbroker and an Ohio doctor, resulted in a group of other problem drinkers coming together to publish a book called *Alcoholics Anonymous*. This publication was the first step in the modern development of a theory of alcoholism as a disease. The ideas had in fact existed for a long time, predating even the Swedish doctor Magnus Huss who coined the term 'alcoholism' in 1849. This time, however, as Shaw (1982 and 1978) points out, the theory was presented in a way that synthesised a sympathetic response to the individual drinker together with a heavily moralistic component.

AA's theory of alcoholism got everyone 'off the hook' as far as the responsibility for problem drinking was concerned. Society is 'off the hook' because, if the disease theory of alcoholism is correct, then governments cannot be expected to make access to alcohol more difficult or to outlaw its production when it clearly only creates problems for a minority of people who have the 'disease'. The vast majority of drinkers are equally relieved, not only of any responsibility for those with problems, but also because they can continue to drink with impunity, safe in the knowledge that only those with the 'disease' will get into trouble from their drinking. The disease theory also lets the problem drinker 'off the hook'. If one has a disease, one is ill and cannot be responsible for the progress of the condition.

In some ways, the idea of alcoholism being a disease had a beneficial influence in its earliest stages: it enabled a move away from the previous viewpoint, i.e. that those who drank to excess were moral degenerates, 'ne'er-do-wells', whose lack of fibre had led them into the ways of the devil. This early advantage of increased compassion was, however, quickly outweighed by the disadvantage of attributing a sick-role medical model approach to a long-term stigmatised condition, which has wide implications for the individual socially and psychologically. The classic understanding of the 'sick role' (Parsons 1951) means that sympathy, acceptance and understanding of the sick person are contingent with certain obligations. Among the most important of these is that the individual will comply with medical treatment and will ultimately 'get well'. Tuckett (1977) points out that certain sufferers from 'long-term stigmatised' conditions cannot qualify for the beneficial effects of 'sick role' status, in that they resist medical treatment or simply cannot get it because it is unavailable. In addition, conditions such as alcoholism and problem drinking are intimately involved in society's attitudes to morality, politics and religion, and those seen to break the rules are stigmatised and viewed as blameworthy.

A further, perhaps more subtle, disadvantage of perceiving problem drinking as an illness or disease is that it affects the manner in which individuals may come to view themselves and the substance. People who see themselves as ill are encouraged to take little or no responsibility for their plight. If, as is the case with the 'disease' theory, the interaction between physiology and alcohol is seen as inevitably producing a catastrophic series of events, then pessimism and a fatalistic response will become widespread, not only among those perceived as 'victims' but also in those struggling to understand the problem. This was typified in the Jellinek formula (Jellinek 1960) which saw a plunge to the 'rock bottom' of dependence as a necessary prerequisite to the long climb back to sobriety (Fig.1.1).

Polich *et al.* (1981), discussing the Jellinek formation of alcohol problems, point out that

> 'a particularly important aspect of the traditional conception of alcoholism is the assumption that the disease typically progresses through a series of definite stages. The identification of these phases of what was learned to be an illness was based to a large extent on the anecdotal and retrospective accounts of members of Alcoholics Anonymous in the 1940s'.

In some senses, the theory of alcoholism as a disease with immutable stages of development, which are inevitable and outside the control of the individual, has been so widely disseminated that many writers now question whether the theory itself may produce the self-reports of behaviour clearly falling into the described pattern. Similar questions have been posed in relation to the mythology surrounding narcotic drug withdrawal. Laurie (1981) draws our attention to the influence of the 'junkie culture' in perpetuating myths about the effects of drugs and the agonies of withdrawal (Fig.1.2).

Similarly, it may be postulated that when a problem drinker enters the 'subculture' of Alcoholics Anonymous, or accepts a medical model explanation of what has happened to them, they may, implicitly, also be accepting a set of behavioural responses which they must display in order to fall into line with the explicit theory.

The changing concept of dependence

Although the 'substance' and 'person/disease' theories of dependence have been pervasive in their influence, at every level of the drug and alcohol field attitudes have been consistently changing. Perhaps the most significant challenges have come first in the alcohol field from the

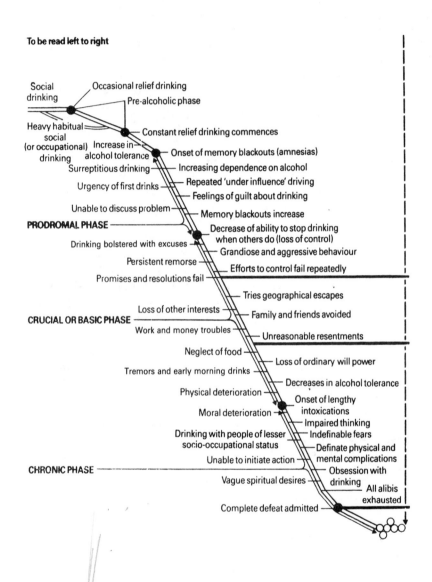

Figure 1.1 *Glatt's chart of alcohol dependence and recovery*

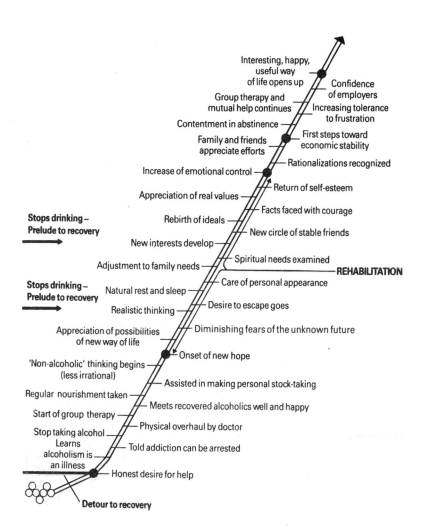

Interesting, happy, useful way of life opens up

Confidence of employers

Group therapy and mutual help continues

Increasing tolerance to frustration

Contentment in abstinence

First steps toward economic stability

Family and friends appreciate efforts

Increase of emotional control

Rationalizations recognized

Return of self-esteem

Appreciation of real values

Facts faced with courage

Rebirth of ideals

New circle of stable friends

New interests develop

Adjustment to family needs

Spiritual needs examined

Stops drinking – Prelude to recovery

REHABILITATION

Care of personal appearance

Natural rest and sleep

Stops drinking – Prelude to recovery

Desire to escape goes

Realistic thinking

Appreciation of possibilities of new way of life

Diminishing fears of the unknown future

'Non-alcoholic' thinking begins (less irrational)

Onset of new hope

Regular nourishment taken

Assisted in making personal stock-taking

Start of group therapy

Meets recovered alcoholics well and happy

Stop taking alcohol

Physical overhaul by doctor

Learns alcoholism is an illness

Told addiction can be arrested

Honest desire for help

Detour to recovery

Source: Heather N., Robertson J. (1985). *Problem Drinking*. London: Penguin

Individual + expectations

Encounter with drugs
and with pervading myths
and beliefs of subculture

Takes on board	*Behaviour*
Drugs + myths = lifestyle	falls
Junkie image	into line
and subculture	with beliefs

Figure 1.2

more behaviourally orientated psychologists. One of the major tenets of the 'person/disease' theory is the irreversible nature of dependence. Once physiologically dependent, the only way to control the disease, because one could never defeat it, was total abstinence. The evidence from work carried out by Davies (1962), and later Heather and Robertson (1981), clearly demonstrated that a minority of problem drinkers could show all the accepted signs of dependent drinking and yet, following behavioural treatment, could return to 'controlled' or social drinking.

Social learning theory

Social learning theories suggest that throughout our lives, and particularly throughout our childhood, we learn to behave in certain ways. This learning takes place through communication and observation, and will therefore be variable, dependent as it is on our environment and its many different influences.

This theory, which has much in common with earlier classical behaviourist theories, suggests that people learn to have certain expectations of substances such as drugs and alcohol. These expectations are founded in the experience that the use of the substance will provide a pleasant consequence or avoid an unpleasant one. Consequences of using the substances, particularly legal ones, are learned from parents, advertisements, peers, books, films and the media generally. In the case of drugs most commonly encountered in everyday life, such as alcohol and tobacco, our expectations are more likely to be based on direct experience.

The question always posed in any study of dependence is why some people go on to problems such as heavier drinking or addictive drug misuse, and others do not. Many writers now feel that the desire to reduce or avoid anxiety is a powerful motivator in dependence behaviour. Learning via a number of situational and psychological 'cues' that drinking heavily or taking drugs can lead to a very satisfactory reduction in anxiety and frustration is a strong reinforcer for the continuance of the dependence behaviour. In time, as Heather *et al.* (1985) suggest, physiological adaptive mechanisms develop to retain homeostasis, and we witness the phenomenon of tolerance and physical withdrawal. There is now great debate about the importance of these adaptive mechanisms in relation to dependence, and it is beyond the scope of this book to examine them fully. However, many popularly held beliefs about the distinction between social, psychological and dependent drinking are facing rigorous examination, and the importance given to certain 'classic' signs and symptoms of dependence may in the light of future research need to be revised.

The social, psychological and cultural context

Another major challenge to traditional theories of substance misuse has come in the past few years from increased research in the drug abuse field. It is becoming more and more evident that clinging to the notion of 'bad' drugs, and seeing illegal drug use as something separate and unconnected with the wider historical and present social context, is simply unhelpful. Gossop (1982):

> 'The comfortable but quite mistaken orthodoxy insists that the 'normal' people who make up the majority of society do not use drugs: set in sharp contrast to this sober normality are the 'abnormal' minority who do.'

This mythology of drug use has been seriously challenged in recent years, along with the 'substance' and 'disease' theories of dependence.

An important contribution in the campaign to combat the mythology of drug misuse came in the somewhat surprising shape of the Vietnam War. Opiate drug use was common among the American troops in Vietnam. Away from home, lonely, bored and often frightened, they could not even draw on support from home, as the war was far from popular throughout the Western world. In this social context, some estimates claim that as many as half the troops took opiates on at least one occasion. Up to 20% or more of the troops felt that they were addicted, and an even greater proportion used a whole range of illegal drugs such as heroin, barbiturates and amphetamines regularly. The speed of the American withdrawal from Vietnam is now a matter of history, but at the time it raised enormous problems. The possibility of many thousands of drug-addicted young men, trained to kill, craving their drugs on the streets of America, was a daunting prospect. However, as Robins (1974) makes clear from an extensive follow-up study, this was simply not the case. Less than 1% of those who felt they were addicted to opiates in Vietnam continued to use them in an addictive fashion following their return to the USA. Only 7% of those addicted prior to return had used opiates at all since their return. These findings fly in the face of the 'substance' theory of drug misuse, and clearly underline that the context in which drug misuse takes place, combined with the psychological state of the user, is all-important in determining the nature of the experience.

Drug use and misuse as a 'career'

Other social scientists and professional researchers, notably Dorn *et al.* (1985), have developed a concept of drug abuse taking on the developmental character of a career. This notion is widely used in two contexts; firstly, as a means of describing the movement from initial use into dependent use of alcohol or drugs:

initial offer (usually from members of peer group)
experimental use
regular recreational use
dependent use/physical or psychological dependence

Pearson *et al.* (1985), in a study of young people and heroin in the north of England, clearly describe how at any stage of the progression from the initial offer to further use of the drug, personal or social variables are at play in deciding which course the young person will follow.

The second important aspect of this concept of drug use as a 'career' involves the tremendous amount of work involved in getting supplies or raising money to obtain supplies. In many ways this is equally applicable to alcohol, where heavy users are constantly 'employed' in concern over financial aspects of their use. This phenomenon of the substitution of dependent behaviour for a socially acceptable career was vividly described by Preble and Casey (1969) in their article 'Taking care of business'. Preble and Casey maintain that, for many lower class heroin users, the use of the drug does not constitute an escape from life, but on the contrary: 'the brief moments of euphoria after each administration of a small amount of heroin constitute a small fraction of their daily lives. The rest of the time they are pursuing a career that is exciting, challenging and rewarding'. There is now a growing body of opinion among researchers in the United Kingdom who, like fellow researchers in the United States, believe that the link between dependence or misuse of drugs and alcohol can no longer be glossed over by claiming that dependency has similar effects on all classes to the same extent. The old adage that drugs and alcohol are no respecter of persons and that dependence is not class-related is sounding hollow in the face of increasing research evidence to the contrary: see Plant *et al.* (1985), Parker *et al.* (1986).

The 'person centred' approach

Whilst all the aforementioned explanations of drug dependency and misuse are enlightening for any professional worker, we believe that the focus of the work of nurses in this field should be on the client, not on the substance. As in all other areas of nursing, it is the individual nature of the client, that essential uniqueness, with which the nurse must form a therapeutic alliance. The difference in working with individuals who are using drugs to deal with personal or social problems is that often (although not always) before tackling the original problems, the nurse must work with the client towards overcoming the dependency problem.

To sum up this first chapter by emphasising the personal and uniquely person-centred nature of dependency, three case histories of typical dependent clients are presented.

Case history – heroin abuse

John is 20 years old and unemployed. He lives in the north of England on a run-down council estate.

John first started to use illegal drugs when he was 16 years old, and originally smoked cannabis for around 12 months. Prior to that, his only other drug use had been legal drugs such as tobacco (occasionally) and alcohol which he would drink when alone with friends at weekends. After 12 months' recreational use of cannabis, John was offered heroin by a member of his peer group who used it occasionally when cannabis was in short supply. John liked the effect that he obtained from smoking heroin and soon it had become his main drug of abuse. At the time of his admission to a local treatment unit, John was smoking a quarter of a gram daily. John had never injected the drug and has not used any other drugs.

Because he is unemployed, John is forced to finance his habit by criminal activity, and usually obtains his money for the drug by petty crime such as shoplifting or small-scale housebreaking. Much of his time is taken up in 'fencing' the goods he has stolen, and then going to see his regular dealer for his supply of heroin. On odd occasions, his dealer has not been able to obtain sufficient supplies and John is forced to visit the local city to 'score' or to obtain his daily supply of the drug.

John lives alone with his mother, his father having died from heart disease when John was 15. John's mother works part-time as a doctor's receptionist and the rest of her time is well filled by looking after John's two younger sisters who are still at school. Money is in short supply, and since the death of John's father the family has had difficulty making ends meet.

John's mother has never quite got over her husband's early death, and John feels she is still depressed and withdrawn to some extent. John feels very guilty for not supporting and helping her more and for bringing her all the trouble and worry of having a son on heroin who is also often in trouble with the police.

John finds it difficult to talk to his mother about his problems because he feels she has so many of her own. Following his father's death, John's work at school deteriorated rapidly and within a year he was smoking cannabis on a regular basis. Prior to this time, he had been seen as a promising pupil and teachers and his parents had hoped he would do well in examinations.

At present John is in a treatment unit awaiting a court case for shoplifting. He finds it extremely difficult to express himself, particularly on an emotional level, and displays a high level of anxiety. His relationship with his mother has deteriorated further.

Case history – alcohol dependence

Margaret is 42 years old and works as a shop assistant. Her home is a small rented flat in a town centre in a 'reasonable' area of Cheshire.

Margaret was born and brought up in the town where she still lives. Her parents are now both dead, having died within a year of each other about five years ago. Margaret has an older brother and two younger sisters. Her early life she describes as fairly uneventful; she did not do particularly well at school and, on leaving at 15, commenced work in a local office. Margaret disliked the isolation of working with a machine all day and changed to shop work, which she finds very stimulating as she enjoys the contact with people.

At 21, Margaret found she was pregnant, and subsequently married her boyfriend Martin. The first child was born shortly after the marriage, while they were living with Margaret's parents because of financial difficulties. Within a couple of years another daughter had arrived, and the family moved into a pleasant semidetached house on a new estate. Martin was a sales representative and was rapidly promoted to a well-paid senior job. Margaret had left her job to look after the children. Every weekend, Margaret's mother would look after the girls while Martin and Margaret went out for a drink to a local club with friends. Margaret did not really enjoy these times; it seemed as though she had nothing to talk about except her experiences with the babies. Other women, wives of Martin's friends, had either chosen a career or managed to combine the two and seemed more interesting to Margaret. She began to feel resentful of her position at home and rows started. During this time, she had begun to 'treat herself' when she was feeling low with the odd bottle of wine from the supermarket. Soon this was a part of her daily experience, and she found it more and more difficult to cope with the demands of the day without feeling depressed and guilty.

Relations deteriorated rapidly between Margaret and Martin and eventually Margaret found that he was having an affair with a female colleague. Her drinking worsened in response to this, and eventually Martin left the family home to continue his new relationship. By this time Margaret was 35 and the children had reached their teens. Although the children were no longer dependent on Margaret and certainly not stopping her from getting a job, she was by now incapable of doing so, and probably unemployable.

Margaret's drinking progressed at an alarming rate and, without the income previously coming into the home, she was soon in financial trouble and was forced to sell the house and move to a rented flat.

Within a month of moving to the flat, Margaret became so despondent that she took an overdose of Valium washed down by huge quantities of wine. She was transferred from the general ward to the alcohol treatment unit following a chat to the nursing staff and psychiatrist.

Case history – tranquilliser abuse

Emily is 72 years old. She is retired, and lives in sheltered accommodation for the elderly in a northern industrial city.

Emily is a former mill worker who lost her husband ten years ago. She has two children, a son aged 40 and a daughter aged 37, both married. Emily would like to see more of them and her five grandchildren, but their jobs have entailed them moving to the south and it is difficult to get together except for holidays.

Six years ago Emily had a slight stroke, following which she found it increasingly difficult to manage in her own home, and so was pleased when the offer of sheltered, warden-controlled accommodation came her way. However, after the move, Emily began to miss the neighbours and the work she had had to do in the house. In the sheltered accommodation, the flats were small and functional, not requiring much cleaning. Each week, the council gardener came to look after the lovely gardens. Emily felt isolated and useless, even at times abandoned by her children, who seemed delighted that she had given up the house. She stopped eating and refused to get out of bed. The doctor prescribed antidepressants and tranquillisers. Emily found that after about three weeks she was feeling much better. The tranquillisers helped her to sleep, and often she would double the dose to get a better effect. After a while, if Emily felt down during the day, she would double the doses of her tablets and doze off – feeling much better afterwards. She found that if she took a little whisky also at night, she slept even more soundly.

Although Emily was running out of her tablets faster than she should have done, she had no trouble obtaining them – the warden simply asked for repeat prescriptions when she went to the doctor's for other people in the block.

The crisis came after about eight months when Emily, in a drugged state, fell over a small coffee table and fractured her collar bone. When the warden found her she thought Emily might have had another stroke as her speech was very slurred. Eventually, the cause was recognised and Emily was referred for help.

Conclusion

These case studies are intended to bring home to the reader the very diverse and personal nature of dependence. Each of these individuals was misusing a different chemical substance, but it is apparent that their cases have certain similarities despite age differences and the legality or illegality of the substance.

It is essential that nurses working with individuals suffering from problems of substance abuse listen carefully for the meaning that the substance has in the person's life and the function it is serving. The nurse must become aware of the primary problem of substance abuse, which, if pursued, goes on to mask all the underlying issues the client needs to tackle.

REFERENCES

Alterman A. I. (1985). *Substance Abuse and Psychotherapy.* New York: Plenum Press.

Davies D. L. (1962). Normal drinking in recovered alcohol addicts. *Quarterly Journal of Studies on Alcohol,* 23, 94–104.

DHSS (1982). *Treatment and Rehabilitation.* Report of the Advisory Council on the Misuse of Drugs. London: HMSO.

DHSS (1983). *Prevention.* Report of the Advisory Council on the Misuse of Drugs. London: HMSO.

Dorn N., Robertson I., Davies P. (1985). The Misuse of Alcohol: Crucial Issues in Dependency Treatment and Prevention. Beckenham: Croom Helm.

Faugier J. (1986). The changing concept of dependence in the drug and alcohol field. *Nursing Practice,* 1, Part 4, 253–6.

Fishburne P. M., Abelson H. I., Cisin I. (1980). *National Survey on Drug Abuse; Main Findings.* Rockville, MD: National Institute on Drug Abuse.

Glatt H. M., Marks J. (1982). *The Dependence Phenomenon.* Lancaster: MPT.

Gossop M. (1982). *Living with Drugs.* London: Temple Smith.

Heather N., Robertson J. (1981). *Controlled Drinking.* London: Methuen.

Heather N., Robertson J. (1985). *Problem Drinking.* London: Penguin.

Hofman F. G. (1983). *A Handbook on Drug and Alcohol Abuse – The Biomedical Aspects.* Oxford: OUP.

Judson H. F. (1974). *Heroin Addiction in Britain.* New York: Harcourt Brace Jovanovich.

Laurie P. (1981). *Drugs – Medical, Psychological and Social Facts.* Harmondsworth: Penguin.

Parker H. J., Bakx K., Newcombe R. (1986). *Drug Misuse in Wirral: A study of eighteen hundred problem drug users.* Liverpool: Liverpool University Press.

Parsons T. (1951). *The Social System.* London: Routledge Kegan Paul.

Pearson G., Gilman M., McIver S. (1985). *Young People and Heroin Use in the North of England.* London: Health Education Council.

Peele S. (1985). *The Meaning of Addiction.* Lexington Books.

Plant M. A., Peck D. F., Samuel E. (1985). *Alcohol, Drugs and School Leavers.* London: Tavistock.

Polich J. M., Armor D. J., Bracker H. B. (1981). *The Course of Alcoholism Four Years after Treatment.* Chichester: John Wiley.

Preble E., Casey J.J. (1969). Taking care of business – the heroin user's life on the street. *International Journal of Addiction,* 4(1), 1–24.

Relman A. S. (1982). Marijuana and health. *New England Journal of Medicine,* 306, 603–5.

Robins L. N. (1974). *The Vietnam Drug User Returns.* Washington: US Government Printing Office.

Scheff T. J. (1967). *Mental Illness and Social Processes.* Harper and Row.
Shaw S. (1982). What is problem drinking? In *Drinking and Problem Drinking.* (Plant M.A., ed.) Junction Books.
Shaw S., Cartwright A., Spratley T., Harwin J. (1978). *Responding to Drinking Problems.* London: Croom Helm.
Tuckett D. (1977). *An Introduction to Medical Sociology.* London: Tavistock.

Chapter 2

The effects of drugs and solvents

Any book focusing upon drug and alcohol dependency needs to include in it some factual information regarding the effects of drugs and alcohol. Throughout this book we look at these substances mainly in relation to the person with the problem. However, in order to provide readers with an easy reference guide to the effects of drugs and alcohol, we have chosen a slightly different format in this chapter and in Chapter 3. We begin by giving a series of definitions provided by the World Health Organisation and then describe the effects of a variety of drugs.

When we consider drug dependence and the effects of drugs (including alcohol), the precise chemistry of the substance is often less significant than the intentions and expectations of the user. In addition, society's view of the drug (for example its legal status) will have considerable implications as to the consequences for the user. In a drug-orientated society there is seldom any attempt to compare the experiences of the person dependent upon opiates to the middle-aged woman dependent upon tranquillisers.

The consumption of all psychoactive drugs can best be viewed as a continuum ranging from ceremonial use, through intermittent social use, use that facilitates functioning, regular continuous use, and in some cases, to a situation where the individual's life revolves around the need to take the drug. Other social activities are relegated to second place. As outlined in Chapter 1, certain terms are commonly used in relation to drugs, and the World Health Organisation (1973) definitions given below help to clarify them.

Drug: a drug is any substance that when taken into a living organism may modify one or more of its functions. It includes not only medications primarily for the treatment of illness, but other pharmacologically active substances.

Drug dependence: a state, psychic and sometimes also physical, resulting from the interaction between a living organism and a drug, characterised by behavioural and other responses that always include a compulsion to take the drug on a continuous basis in order to experience its psychic effects, and sometimes to avoid the discomfort of its absence. Tolerance may or may not be present.

Dependence-producing drug: a drug that has the capacity to interact with a living organism to produce a state of psychic or physical dependence or both.

Physical dependence: an adaptive state that manifests itself by intense physical disturbances when administration of the drug is suspended or when its action is affected by the administration of a specific antagonist. The physical withdrawal symptoms referred to vary from drug to drug, and their relief by continued use of the drug plays a critical part.

Tolerance: the way the body adapts to repeated ingestion of the drug; the effect of the drug becomes lessened and thus higher doses are required to maintain the same effect.

Cross-tolerance: may occur between drugs that are pharmacologically linked.

Addiction: dependence upon the drug has developed to a stage where effects and complications of use are having serious detrimental consequences for the individual and society.

Given possible problems associated with the legal status and effects of particular drugs (both immediate or longer term), drug takers may well experience detrimental consequences even without psychological and/or physical dependence (more commonly in the absence of physical dependence). The term 'problem drug-taker' describes the person whose drug use results in social, psychological, physical or legal problems associated with dependence, intoxication or regular excessive use. Drug 'abuse' or drug 'misuse' reflects the observer's view that the drug-taking is harmful or socially unacceptable.

'Recreational' drug use describes the use of drugs for pleasure, as distinct from dependent or functional use – it remains a controversial term!

This chapter outlines the effects of drugs and reviews their patterns of use. The drugs described are central nervous system depressants (hypnosedatives, minor tranquillisers, solvents and gases), central nervous system stimulants (amphetamine, cocaine and caffeine), hallucinogens (LSD, hallucinogenic mushrooms and cannabis) and opiates. Although alcohol is also a central nervous system depressant, we feel that the effects and patterns of use are such that it requires separate consideration (see Chapter 3).

CENTRAL NERVOUS SYSTEM DEPRESSANTS

Certain drugs have a sedative and tranquillising effect upon the central nervous system (CNS) and these include alcohol, hypnosedatives, minor tranquillisers and solvents or gases. Alcohol is described in Chapter 3.

Hypnosedatives

Hypnosedatives are medically used for their sedative and hypnotic effect. The two most common groups in this category are the barbiturates and the sedatives (chlormethiazole and chloral hydrate).

Barbiturates

Barbiturates are produced from barbituric acid, which was discovered in 1864. Since 1903 a large number of synthetic derivatives have been produced under a variety of trade names. Within the barbiturate group there are some drugs that are extremely short-acting and show their sedative effect shortly after ingestion. These are most often misused because of their intoxicating effect (e.g. Tuinal, Seconal, Nembutal). Longer-acting barbiturates are slower to have their effect and are very gradually accepted by the body. They are more commonly used in the treatment of epilepsy.

Patterns of use: barbiturates became extremely popular at street level during the 1960s when they were combined with amphetamine and marketed as Drinamyl ('purple hearts'). Prior to this development, they were commonly used in medical practice for the suppression of epileptic fits, e.g. phenobarbitone (Nembutal), as a short-acting anaesthetic, e.g. thiopentone (Pentothal) and as sedatives and hypnotics. These medical uses continue to some extent, but it is noteworthy that prescriptions for barbiturates have dropped from 16 million in 1966 in England and Wales to fewer than 3 million in 1980 in England (Committee on the Review of Medicines 1979). The most common source of supply of barbiturates is through their diversion between factory production and pharmacy delivery, or their illegal sale following prescribing.

Barbiturates were particularly popular in combination with CNS stimulants. The user would get a 'snort' of amphetamine sulphate and a short while later, in order to present some semblance of normal behaviour to friends or family, would take a barbiturate. Throughout the 1970s barbiturates were easily available on the illicit drug market, and such were the consequences that City Roads was set up in London in the late 1970s (Jamieson *et al.* 1984). Whilst changes in prescribing practices have reduced their availability, barbiturates continue to be a serious problem amongst heavy multiple drug users. Nembutal and Tuinal are the barbiturates found most frequently in the illicit drug market.

Legal status: under the Medicines Act, all sedatives and hypnotics are 'prescription only' and can therefore only be sold by a pharmacist on the basis of a doctor's prescription. Since January 1985, all the 'misusable' barbiturates were included in Class B of the Misuse of Drugs Act.

Route of administration and cost: barbiturates are powders made into tablets, coloured capsules, ampoules and soluble form. For their short-term medical use the drug may be injected, but oral ingestion in tablet form is common. Amongst drug users, they are often taken in combination with alcohol but may be taken injected. Tuinal is available at about £1 for two capsules which would be sufficient to intoxicate a non-user (Institute for the Study of Drug Dependence 1985).

Effects: by depressing the CNS, a small dose of barbiturates will make people feel relaxed and less anxious. The effect is similar to that of a small amount of alcohol. As the dose is increased the recipient becomes more intoxicated and sedated. However, there is also a likelihood that depression, hostility or anxiety may develop.

The physical effects seen if the person remains awake under the influence of barbiturates are general clumsiness, slurring of speech, confusion and mental instability. Large overdoses cause death from respiratory failure, and the effects are potentiated if alcohol or other depressant drugs have been taken.

Injecting barbiturates produces the desired effects almost immediately. Barbiturate injectors are at risk of overdose, abscesses at the site of injection and complications because of poor injection technique, e.g. septicaemia and hepatitis. If barbiturates are used regularly, tolerance and psychological dependence are likely to occur. Chronic intoxication with barbiturates can lead to impairment of mental ability, confusion and increased emotional instability. Long-term heavy users have an increased susceptibility to bronchitis and pneumonia as the cough reflex is depressed.

The abstinence syndrome is the most characteristic and distinguishing feature of dependence upon barbiturates. It begins within 24 hours after the cessation of drug taking, reaching its peak of intensity in two to three days and subsiding slowly. The symptoms present include anxiety, involuntary muscle twitching, tremor of the hands, progressive weakness, dizziness, visual perception distortions, nausea, vomiting, sleeplessness and a fall in blood pressure. If the symptoms are not treated, convulsions and a delirious state, similar to delirium tremens, can occur. Sudden withdrawal from high doses can be fatal.

Sedatives

Chlormethiazole (Heminevrin) is a prescription-only sedative and is sometimes used in the treatment of insomnia because of its freedom from hangover. It is used in the treatment of acute withdrawal symptoms from alcohol, but to minimise risk of dependence administration should be limited to nine days, under inpatient supervision (BNF 1986). Details of specific effects and prescribing advice are given in Chapter 4.

Chloral hydrate is a prescription-only sedative used in the treatment of insomnia in the elderly. Doses are taken well diluted in order to minimise gastrointestinal disturbances.

Minor tranquillisers

Tranquillisers can be divided into two groups – minor and major tranquillisers. Major tranquillisers are used in the treatment of severe mental disorders, and although there is concern about their use, serious difficulties in respect of physical or psychological dependence are unlikely.

The most commonly prescribed minor tranquillisers are the benzodiazepines. They are not only used as tranquillisers to allay anxiety but also as an hypnotic to induce sleep, a relaxant to relieve muscle tension and as an anticonvulsant in the treatment of epilepsy.

The benzodiazepines were first introduced in 1960, with chlordiazepoxide (Librium) being recommended for the treatment of anxiety. This was followed in 1963 by the marketing of diazepam (Valium). They were soon seen as a safe alternative to the barbiturates, whose pattern of abuse was becoming apparent. The benzodiazepines were considered to be more effective in the treatment of anxiety and to be safer if taken as an overdose. It also appeared that they were relatively free from side effects, and until recently risks associated with long-term use were not evident. Modern sedatives promised a relief in tension whilst not causing daytime drowsiness.

A wide variety of benzodiazepines is marketed, and the most commonly prescribed are diazepam (Valium), chlordiazepoxide (Librium), lorazepam (Ativan), oxazepam (Serenid), nitrazepam (Mogadon) and flurazepam (Dalmane). Formulations are determined by relative potency and determination of half-life. The half-lives vary greatly, e.g. diazepam 100 hours, oxazepam 12 hours. Short-acting benzodiazepines are used in the treatment of acute anxiety, whilst the longer-acting ones are likely to be used for their hypnotic qualities.

Patterns of use: the prescribing of benzodiazepines has increased consistently since they were first marketed. Such increases were enhanced until recently by the widespread acceptance of these drugs, by the public and the medical profession. Lader (1978) in his commentary describes them as the 'opium of the masses'. Several researchers including Parish (1971) and Williams (1981) have shown a consistent increase in the number of prescriptions for tranquillisers, the majority of which are for benzodiazepines. Unfortunately we do not know the dose or duration of the prescription. A considerable number of benzodiazepines are given as repeat prescriptions by general practitioners (Marks 1983).

A national household survey in the USA in the early 1970s found that 13% of men and 29% of women had been prescribed a tranquilliser in the previous year (Parry *et al.* 1973). Some work by Balter *et al.* (1974) focused upon the use of sedative drugs in Europe, when national samples of individuals in nine Western European countries were asked about sedative drug use. The UK, Denmark, Netherlands and Belgium were at the top, with about 8% of the adult population using sedative drugs. The examination of prescribing in general practice reveals that psychotropic drugs were prescribed more often than any other group, accounting for 17% of prescriptions (Skegg *et al.* 1977). An unpublished survey in southeast London revealed that 9% of the adult male population and 19% of females received a prescription for at least one psychotropic drug (Petursson and Lader 1984).

Whilst the majority of benzodiazepine prescriptions are for a short time period, considerable numbers of people – 27% of those prescribed benzodiazepines according to Parish (1971) – are receiving the drugs longer term. The view of Marks (1983) is reinforced, since psychotropic drugs lead the list of repeat prescriptions.

Twice as many females as males are prescribed tranquillisers. Women who are retired or unemployed and not in the direct labour force are high consumers, and the elderly receive twice as many prescriptions for psychotropic drugs as do younger people. Horwitz (1977) concluded that women 'accept the self label of psychiatric illness more readily than men'. Such labels are reinforced by the style of advertising by the drug companies and perhaps, until recently, the predominance of men in general practice.

Legal status: all tranquillisers are prescription only under the Medicines Act.

Route of administration: benzodiazepines are manufactured as powders and formed into capsules or tablets which are taken by mouth. They are also available in injecting form, when they are used for acute medical or psychiatric conditions.

Effects: the most common effects are to depress mental alertness and activity whilst not leaving the person drowsy to the extent that barbiturates do. They create a general reduction in anxiety and assist in the relief of tension, but are devoid of antidepressant or analgesic effects. Whilst in some situations these effects are welcome, the less pleasant effects include a reduced reaction time, impaired powers of observation, lessened manual dexterity, memory loss and inevitably lowered efficiency when driving motor vehicles or using machinery. The type and duration of effect is dependent upon the user's past experience of the drug and on the half-life of the drug.

Chronic intoxication can lead to dysarthria, ataxia, nystagmus and affective lability. The effects upon mood, sexual behaviour, sociability and aggression are probably influenced by the expectation of the user.

Long-term use of a benzodiazepine increases the risk of physical and psychological dependence. The physical withdrawal syndrome varies, but gradual reduction of the drug is likely to reduce the severity of withdrawal symptoms. Whilst there is much debate as to the optimal period for prescribing these drugs, withdrawal symptoms may follow a very short period of treatment, i.e. four to six weeks (Murphy *et al.* 1984). Tyrer *et al.* (1981) reported that withdrawal phenomena are related to the rate at which the drugs are excreted and metabolised, being milder in slowly eliminated compounds (i.e. those with a long half-life). Rebound insomnia has been reported following withdrawal of short-acting drugs. Symptoms include sleep disturbance, irritability, increased tension and anxiety, panic attacks, hand tremor, profuse sweating, difficulty in concentration, dry retching, nausea, weight loss, palpitations, headache, muscular pain and stiffness. The withdrawal symptoms are particularly present following use of short-acting benzodiazepines, e.g. lorazepam, temazepam. The desire to start to use the drug again is great, since the withdrawal syndrome often closely resembles the original reason for prescribing. The symptoms usually emerge following a reduction in dosage.

Solvents and gases

Solvent sniffing, popularly known as 'glue sniffing', is the practice of inhaling the vapours of a chemical substance through the nose or mouth to produce an altered state of mind. Glue is just one of a large range of chemical substances used; the most common are:

1. *Adhesives* – the impact adhesives are the best known examples in this group as they contain toluene and acetone. Cellulose paint thinners and nail polish remover also contain these substances.
2. *Dry cleaning materials* – many household (as well as commercial) products are used; the active ingredients involved are trichloro-ethylene, trichlorethane and carbon tetrachloride.
3. *Aerosols* – hair lacquers, window cleaners and spray paints are common in this group. The effects are contained in the gas propellants, e.g. fluorohydrocarbons.
4. *Fuels* – these include camping gases and lighter fuel, which contain tetraethyl lead.

In order to increase the effect of the substance, attempts are made to increase the concentration of the vapour by sniffing inside a plastic bag.

Patterns of use: solvent misuse has been known as a serious and developing problem in Britain since the early 1960s and in America since the 1950s. We can go back as far as 1799 when 'laughing gas' was abused in the dentist's chair! Deliberate sniffing of glue from model aeroplane kits began as early as 1940 (Rogers 1982), and in industries where hydrocarbon chemicals were used, many workers developed a psychological dependence. However, concern about the use of solvents in the UK has really developed since the mid-1970s. There are no national surveys that focus upon these issues, but views about the extent of the problem are gathered via the police, social workers and medical professionals who come into contact with misusers. There are some suggestions that for many adolescents use of solvents is a short-lived experimental exercise, although there exists a much smaller group who continue to use after the fad has passed amongst their peers.

A Scottish survey showed those who continue to use come from an environment where a parent is absent and where there is a history of marital problems (Herzderg and Wolkind 1983). Similar trends have been noted in a study in the West Midlands by Sansum (1984).

Solvent misuse becomes common in a small local area (e.g. a housing estate or school) and is often linked with the onset of long summer evenings. Use gains momentum by midsummer, but slows down as autumn closes in. Sniffing usually takes place in a confined space or an isolated area. Canal bridges, old railway yards and garden sheds are the most popular venues.

Legal status: in Scotland it is an offence to 'recklessly' sell solvents to children knowing that they intend to inhale them. In England and Wales such restrictions do not exist, and the common process whereby misusers come to the attention of the law is through activity associated with the intoxicating effect of the solvent, e.g. breach of the peace. In December 1986 one of the first cases was brought to the courts in London, when a shopkeeper had been found selling correction fluid for typing to young people.

Route of administration: the most common method is by pouring the solvent into a plastic bag and inhaling the fumes. Sometimes a rag or cloth is saturated with the chemical and then sniffed. Aerosols are sprayed into a bag or balloon or directly into the nose or mouth.

Effects: the inhaled vapours are absorbed through the lungs and rapidly reach the brain. They have primarily a depressant effect, and as a result general body functions such as breathing and heart rate are depressed. Repeated and deep inhalations can cause disorientation, loss of control and unconsciousness from which the user usually recovers. Complications arise if the vapour is not removed once the person becomes unconscious, or if the person vomits and inhales the vomit.

Solvent inhalation produces similar effects to early alcohol intoxication, including dizzy feelings, euphoria, disorientation and lack of coordination. Like alcohol, solvents reduce inhibitions and result in boisterous and emotionally labile behaviour. The effects generally last up to half an hour, followed by feelings of nausea and headache. The process of inhalation may be repeated in order to counteract these aftereffects. With larger doses, hallucinatory experiences can occur. Accidental death or injury can happen, especially if inhalation takes place in an unsafe environment such as a roof or canal bank. Inhalation of the stomach contents following unconsciousness can lead to death, as may also happen if the method used to inhale the solvent obstructs breathing (e.g. a large plastic bag placed over the head, or sniffing in a confined space). Most of the deaths in the UK associated with solvents occurred amongst those using the solvent alone.

Some products, especially aerosol gases and cleaning fluids, make the heart more sensitive to the hormone adrenaline, and upon exertion or excitement, cardiac arrhythmia may occur, leading to heart failure and death. Gases such as those present in aerosols or lighter fuel refills squirted into the mouth can cause death through suffocation.

In examining the effects of long-term use, we are faced with scarcity of information. The main work has been completed by Watson (1979) who studied 115 patients referred to her clinic. She found 'no physical or laboratory abnormalities directly attributable to the abuse of solvents'. In one case some bone marrow abnormalities were noted, but further investigations could not be carried out. Watson followed up this study with a review of 400 Scottish cases stretching from 1975 to 1981. Among the referrals, 90% of whom were using adhesives, was an aerosol death, several accidental injuries, temporary kidney and liver damage, but no evidence of lasting harm. However, Fornazzi *et al.* (1983) argue that there is evidence of brain damage from toluene. Ron (1986), having completed a review of the literature, states: 'in the light of present knowledge the possibility that permanent structural brain damage, with accompanying psychiatric manifestations, results from solvent abuse, remains inconclusive'. Tolerance develops amongst solvent users, and after regular use, greater amounts or a greater concentration of the vapour are required in order to achieve the desired effect. Psychological dependence develops in a minority of susceptible users, especially those who have underlying personality or family problems. They are likely to become 'lone sniffers', quite different from those who experiment.

CENTRAL NERVOUS SYSTEM STIMULANTS

Some drugs have properties leading to stimulation of the central nervous system (CNS). The arousal of the sympathetic nervous system promotes those changes needed to meet an emergency and prepares the body to deal with stressful situations – the 'fight or flight' response. Drugs with these properties include amphetamine, cocaine and caffeine.

Amphetamine

This synthetic stimulant was originally developed for medical use, and is sold under a variety of trade names, e.g. Dexedrine, Methedrine. Structurally, amphetamine closely resembles norepinephrine. There are three types: racemic amphetamines (e.g. Benzedrine), dexamphetamines (e.g. Dexedrine) and methylamphetamines (e.g. Methedrine). The three vary greatly in their potency, with the strongest being methylamphetamine. The common street name for amphetamine is 'speed' or 'whiz'.

In addition to the original amphetamine compounds, numerous derivatives have been developed, often including a mixture of stimulants and depressants, e.g. dexamphetamine and amylobarbitone (Drinamyl). The mixture of stimulants and depressants is known as 'dexes', and street terms include 'purple hearts', 'blues' and 'sulphate'.

Amphetamine-like stimulants are also available. These include methyl phenidate (Ritalin), which is a stimulator of the CNS and produces virtually the same effects as amphetamine (though of a slightly lesser magnitude), dose for dose. Street users often describe Ritalin as a 'cleaner high', and it is sometimes used amongst polydrug users to accompany a depressant drug. Diethylpropion is recommended for use in severely obese patients; its main trade names are Tenuate (deleted for use by Merrell in 1981), Tenuate Dospan (known as 'tombstone') and Apisate (with added B vitamins, thiamine and riboflavin). Other amphetamine-like stimulants include pemoline (Kethamed – deleted 1981), Filon (phenmetrazine theoclate with phenbutrazate hydrochloride) and Durophet-M (racemic and dexamphetamine with methaqualone). These are the latterday equivalent of the 1960s 'purple hearts'.

Patterns of use: amphetamines have been used in medical practice since the mid-1930s, mainly as appetite suppressants and as a symptomatic antidepressant. In recent years, their general use has been discouraged and they are now only recommended for the treatment of hyperactive children, as they have a paradoxical effect, and of narcolepsy (a condition where an individual drops suddenly off to sleep several times a day). Some of the milder amphetamine-like drugs are used as short-term appetite suppressants in obesity.

Non-medical use of amphetamines was reported during the Spanish Civil War, when they were given to troops in order to increase their fighting vigour (Tyler 1984). They were also given to troops during

World War II. Gossop (1982) reported Adolf Hitler's use of methylamphetamine from 1938 onwards, and the pattern associated with military strife – the Americans in Korea and Vietnam being amongst the recipients. By the end of this era of generous use, the dangerous effects of the drug and its popularity on the street were finally recognised.

In the UK, amphetamines became very popular during the 'mods' period of the 1960s and this popularity continued into the early 1970s. They were supplied via medical sources and pharmacy burglaries. Despite a decline in conviction and seizure statistics during previous years, the late 1970s saw an increase in use and availability on the illicit market. Recent statistics suggest a considerable increase, which has been confirmed by fieldwork and a fall in price, indicating large quantities on the illicit market. The more common kind of street 'speed' is amphetamine sulphate, which contains equal parts of racemic and dexamphetamine and has the appearance of a whitish crystalline powder.

Amphetamines are used to maintain long periods of performance at manual or intellectual tasks, and also for recreational purposes. The drugs are common in some colleges, studios, construction sites and in the music business.

Route of administration: amphetamines may be taken by mouth, dissolved in water and injected, or smoked. The manufactured powders are generally sniffed.

Illicit amphetamine sulphate retails at about £10 to £15 per gram (20–40% pure – glucose powder is the traditional cut in the UK). An occasional user might take several weeks to consume half a gram, whilst a heavy user who has developed substantial tolerance to the drug's effects might consume 1–2 grams or more a day.

Legal status: all the amphetamines and similar stimulants are prescription-only drugs under the Medicines Act, and many are also controlled under the Misuse of Drugs Act. Patients can possess them if they have been prescribed, otherwise unauthorised production, supply or possession is an offence.

Effects: the action of amphetamines is similar to that of adrenaline, which is naturally produced in the body to deal with emergencies or stress. These adrenaline-like effects include increased heart rate, dilated pupils, increased blood pressure, faster breathing and suppression of appetite. Fatigue is postponed and there is a general increase in alertness, energy and confidence. The effects of a single dose last about 3–4 hours. If no more of the drug is taken, fatigue and mild depression can occur as the effects of the drug wear off.

At high doses, a general feeling of increased physical and mental capacity is evident. High doses taken repeatedly over a few days may lead to delirium ('amphetamine psychosis'), producing panic states, hallucinations and persecutory ideas. This condition will gradually disappear as the level of the drug in the body is reduced. The risk of psychological dependence upon the synthetic stimulants, given their mood-altering capabilities, is considerable. Following cessation of regular use, the user is likely to feel depressed, lethargic and tense, although there is no clear physiological withdrawal syndrome.

Tolerance occurs with regular use of amphetamines, and frequent use of high doses is likely to lead to the presence of delusions, hallucinations and paranoid ideas. These effects are much more likely to occur after injection than after oral ingestion.

Cocaine

This is a powerful, short-lasting CNS stimulant and local anaesthetic. It is derived from *Erythroxylon coca* and other *Erythroxylon* species in South America. Natives in the growing regions of South America, especially the Andes, chew the coca leaf in order to increase their physical strength and endurance. Oral ingestion of cocaine was widespread in the late nineteenth and early twentieth centuries, when it was an ingredient of patent medicines, tonics and soft drinks. Freud believed strongly in the medicinal powers of the drug.

Patterns of use: Andean Indians have probably been chewing coca leaves for thousands of years. The chewer moistens a 'wad' with spit and places it between the cheek and gum. Following the Spanish exploration of South America, coca leaves were transported to Europe, where their impact was minimal.

In Britain, cocaine was restricted under the 1920 Dangerous Drugs Act, following stories of cocaine sniffing amongst British troops. The 1930s saw the British cocaine scene become virtually extinct, soon to be gradually replaced by amphetamine. By the 1960s, cocaine use was largely restricted to heroin addicts, a number of whom received both drugs on prescription. Following the establishment of the drug dependency clinics in 1968, cocaine use and prescription ground almost to a halt.

During the mid-1970s, cocaine increased in popularity and it became associated with glamour, panache and success. The late 1970s and early 1980s have also seen a dramatic increase in use in the United States. In the US, a National Institute on Drug Abuse report stated that the number of people who had tried cocaine at least once had increased from 5.4 million in 1974 to 21.6 million in 1982 (National Institute on Drug Abuse 1984). Recent UK enforcement statistics suggest continued and increased spread of cocaine use (Institute for the Study of Drug Dependence 1986). Common street names for cocaine are 'coke', 'snow' and 'toot'.

Route of administration and cost: cocaine can be (and sometimes is) injected, especially with heroin. The more common method is by sniffing the powder up one nostril at a time, using a small tube such as a straw. It is absorbed into the blood supply via the nasal membranes. 'Freebasing' refers to the less common practice of converting the drug to cocaine hydrochloride so that it can be smoked through a pipe, thus producing a more immediate effect than sniffing. The price of cocaine is £55 to £70 per gram (30–70% pure). The typical casual user might consume a quarter of a gram over several days, whilst regular users might use 1–2 grams per day.

Legal status: cocaine, its various salts and the leaves of the coca plant are controlled in Class A of the Misuse of Drugs Act. It is illegal to produce, possess or supply the drug unless prescribed.

Effects: like amphetamine, cocaine produces physiological arousal accompanied by feelings of exhilaration and a general sense of well-being. The effect begins within a few minutes of nasal ingestion and reaches its peak after 20 minutes. The dose may have to be repeated every 20–30 minutes in order to maintain the desired effect.

At high doses, or if repeated doses are taken over several hours, toxic effects become noticeable, including paranoia, confusion, hypersensitivity and tactile hallucinations. The aftereffects include fatigue and depression, although they are less severe than those of amphetamines.

Whilst neither tolerance nor a physiological withdrawal syndrome are present, there is the risk of strong psychological dependence and the potential aftereffects reinforce the desire to repeat the dose.

A significant number of regular cocaine users develop problems. These include poor sleep patterns, malnutrition, agitation, bouts of paranoia, confusion and mood swings. All these effects diminish and eventually disappear when use is discontinued. Repeated sniffing damages the membranes lining the nose and damage may also occur to the nasal septum. 'Crack' is a smokable form of cocaine derived from cocaine hydrochloride powder. It is produced by freebasing. In the UK, although cocaine may be gaining in popularity, crack is potentially a drug whose popularity, certainly in London (1989), is leading to great concern amongst workers. It may prove to be the challenge of the 1990s.

Caffeine

The most frequently encountered stimulant is caffeine, found in coffee, tea, soft drinks and many analgesics. Coffee is the strongest of the beverages, although a cup of tea can contain almost as much caffeine as instant coffee. About 70% of all UK adults drink coffee and 86% drink tea. With an average of three cups per day for each coffee drinker and four cups a day for each tea drinker, daily caffeine consumption in Britain averages approximately 440 mg per person.

Effects: in moderate doses (150–250 mg) caffeine allays drowsiness and fatigue. It also assists in delaying the onset of sleep and helps to prevent boredom and tiredness. Consumption of 500–600 mg a day can cause feelings of anxiety and restlessness. Tolerance develops to most of the physiological effects of caffeine. A withdrawal syndrome occurs after regular use of about 400 mg per day, consisting of a reduction in alertness, drowsiness and headaches.

HALLUCINOGENS

There is no clear agreement about what these drugs should be called; they are variously known as psychedelics, psychotomimetics and psychotogens. The key difference from other classes of drugs is their ability to alter perceptual function. The substances to be most aware of are synthetic hallucinogens, hallucinogenic mushrooms and cannabis.

Lysergic acid diethylamide

LSD is a white powder, derived from ergot, a fungus found growing on rye and other grasses. It is a very potent drug and only a few micrograms are required for effect. It was isolated from ergot in 1938 and was accidentally ingested by its discoverer (Dr Albert Hofmann) in 1943, who thereby experienced the first 'LSD trip'.

'Last Friday, April 16th, 1943, I was forced to interrupt my work in the laboratory in the middle of the afternoon and proceed home, being affected by a remarkable restlessness, combined with a slight dizziness. At home, I lay down and sank into a not unpleasant intoxicated-like condition, characterised by an extremely stimulated imagination. In a dreamlike state, with eyes closed, I perceived an uninterrupted stream of fantastic pictures, extraordinary shapes with intense kaleidoscopic play of colours. After some two hours, this condition faded away.' (Gossop 1984)

In the 1950s and 1960s, the drug was used to assist in recovery of unconscious and repressed thought and feelings during psychotherapy. The manufacturing company (Sandoz) hoped that it would reveal the secrets of schizophrenia, by producing a 'model psychosis'. By the early 1960s, its use at a therapeutic level had decreased, although its popularity for non-medical purposes, initially in the United States and later in the UK, began to develop. It was particularly popular amongst hippy groups because of its association with special religious and mystical experiences, including a sense of increased creativity and search for new meaning.

LSD is commonly known as 'acid'.

Some synthetic hallucinogens have been produced, such as

phencyclidine (PCP or 'angel dust') and hallucinogenic amphetamines.

Patterns of use: LSD has probably been used by less than 1% of the population, although amongst college students this figure is likely to be higher. Seizures and convictions for LSD offences have increased every year since 1979, but given the great difficulty in detection (since small amounts are easily manufactured), any trend on prevalence and availability is difficult to assess.

Route of administration and cost: the small amount required for a trip is usually mixed with other substances and made into tablets or capsules and then taken by mouth. If the drug is in a solution, it may be taken absorbed on paper, gelatin sheets or sugar cubes.

Today, a single dose of LSD costs about £2. One dose may be sufficient for a mild trip, three or four are necessary for a full-blown hallucinogenic experience.

Legal status: LSD and other hallucinogens (e.g. mescaline, psilocybin) are controlled as Class A of the Misuse of Drugs Act. Special regulations mean that they can only be supplied or possessed for research and other special purposes by a person licensed by the Home Secretary.

Effects: a trip begins about 30 minutes after ingestion, and can last for several hours. The effect can vary greatly and usually fades out after about 12 hours. The experience depends upon dosage and to a great extent the setting. The first sensations include a feeling of excitement and/or agitation, an increased awareness of the body and its motor functions. Perceptual distortions often occur, including intensified colours, distorted shapes, sizes and movement in stationary objects. Emotional reactions vary; usually the underlying mood is exaggerated. Physical effects include dizziness, increased blood pressure, dilation of pupils and relaxation of lung muscle.

Users report that a balanced frame of mind, a familiar place and the company of a friend who knows the drug will help to avoid a bad trip!

There is no reliable evidence to suggest that long-term use of LSD causes brain damage. Some users report short-lived 'flashbacks', briefly reliving a bad trip, which can leave the person anxious, distressed and frightened.

Hallucinogenic mushrooms

A great variety of hallucinogenic plants were used by ancient civilisations to gain access to the spirit world. The UK is endowed with about a dozen types of 'magic mushrooms', whilst the Americas can claim more than one hundred species. Those found in the UK include *Psilocybe semilanceata* (liberty cap) and *Amanita muscaria* (fly agaric). Psychoactive mushrooms of the *Panaeolus* and *Psilocybe* groups contain the hallucinogens psilocybin and psilocin. Present-day use of plant hallucinogens appears to have developed as a legal and more 'organic' alternative to LSD.

Patterns of use: the eating of hallucinogenic mushrooms has been reported as a common event amongst hippies and groups of teenagers, in urban areas of Great Britain and in rural Wales. The most commonly available species is the liberty cap.

Effects: these are said to be very similar to a mild LSD trip, and the type of experience is similarly influenced by the user's mood, environment and expectations. Prominent signs of physiological arousal are evident, as is euphoria. As the dose increases, the prospects of the occurrence of visual distortions and hallucinations becomes greater. This usually takes about 20 to 30 liberty caps.

Bad trips and flashbacks may occur as a result of hallucinogenic mushrooms. However, a greater danger is the risk of picking and eating a poisonous species of *Amanita*. It is difficult to determine any long-term effects of the mushrooms, since few studies have been able to look at the issue in great depth.

Cannabis

Cannabis is derived from *Cannabis sativa*, a green, bushy plant with saw-toothed leaves and fluted stalks, ranging in height from 1 to 6 metres. The male plant produces the tough fibres from which hemp rope is made, whilst the female generates the sticky aromatic resins. The most important psychoactive ingredients are the tetrahydrocannabinols; these are concentrated in the resin. The most common form of cannabis in the UK is hashish, which is resin that has been scraped from the plant and compressed into slabs, chunks, sticky balls or powdery flakes. Cannabis is also used in the form of dried plant material, commonly known as 'marijuana', 'ganja', 'weed' or 'grass'. There are differences between them, however; for example, marijuana should be devoid of seeds and twigs, whilst ganja includes these as well as the leaves and flowering tops.

Five times more concentrated than the resin is hash oil, also known as 'honey oil'. This is produced by boiling finely powdered hash in a solvent such as alcohol and straining out the cellulose solids. The solvents then evaporate, leaving a sticky, greeny-brown oil.

Patterns of use: recreational use of cannabis dates back to the ancient Chinese, who were particularly skilled at the cultivation of the plant. In Britain, the non-medical use of cannabis was prohibited in 1928, after an Egyptian delegate persuaded an international opium conference to include it in an agreement adopted by the UK. From the 1950s, cannabis was popular in the flourishing jazz scene in the clubs of Soho.

Since the 1960s the pros and cons of the legal status of cannabis have been an issue of considerable discussion, debate and polarisation. The 'escalation' syndrome appears to worry some people, that is the fear that use of cannabis will lead to use of heroin. The report in 1968 of a committee chaired by Baroness Wootton stated that there was a 'body of opinion that criticises the present legislative treatment of cannabis on the grounds that it exaggerates the dangers of the drug and needlessly interferes with civil liberty'. However, the views of the media and government were different and cannabis use remained an illegal activity. Use increased during the early 1970s, and after a period of stabilisation increased again in the late 1970s. Most people who take cannabis are between 16 and 30 years old. Nine out of ten seizures of illegal drugs and convictions for drug offences involve cannabis, usually for possession of small amounts.

Route of administration and cost: the preparations available in the UK are generally smoked by rolling the cannabis into a cigarette, combined with tobacco, making a 'joint'. It can also be smoked in a pipe, and the herbal type can be brewed into a drink or put in food. At street level, imported herbal cannabis retails for about £1 per gram, whilst resin costs about 25 pence per gram. About £2 worth of cannabis could be used to make a couple of cannabis cigarettes sufficient for two or three people to get mildly intoxicated. Heavy, regular cannabis consumers might smoke five joints a day, using about 7 grams of resin within a week.

Legal status: cannabis is controlled under the Misuse of Drugs Act which prohibits its medical and non-medical use. Herbal cannabis, cannabis resin and cannabis oil are in Class B of the Act. Active chemical ingredients (cannabinoids) that have been separated from the plant are Class A drugs.

Effects: it must be stressed that the effects depend to a considerable extent on the mood, expectations and social setting of the user. It is quite common not to experience very much at first. The most common basis for using cannabis is to experience its pleasurable effects. These include the development of a state of relaxation, talkativeness, laughter and increased sensory perceptions, especially of sound and colour. However, short-term memory, concentration, intellectual performance and manual dexterity are impaired. As the dose increases, perceptual distortions, forgetfulness and impairment of thought processes may occur. If a person is inexperienced in the use of cannabis and is feeling apprehensive or depressed, severe psychological distress and confusion may develop. The effects of the drug start a few minutes after smoking and may last up to one hour with small doses and several hours with high doses. There is no 'hangover' feeling.

Great controversy exists about the possible consequences of long-term use of cannabis. It is quite likely that frequent inhalation of cannabis smoke over several years increases the risk of bronchitis and other respiratory disorders. Whilst mild withdrawal symptoms have been produced in experiments, a clear physical withdrawal syndrome is not evident. Regular users may develop a psychological need for the drug and seek its use to aid social interaction. An 'amotivational syndrome' characterised by apathy, withdrawal, poor judgement and a lack of achievement has sometimes been associated with long-term use of cannabis. However, such features may have been present prior to drug use and are not uncommon in a person who is chronically intoxicated. Regular, frequent cannabis use during pregnancy may cause premature birth, but results are conflicting.

OPIATES

Opiates (also known as narcotic analgesics) are derived from the opium poppy. They and their synthetic equivalents are sometimes collectively known as opioids.

The naturally occurring opiates include opium, morphine, heroin and codeine. As well as having considerable analgesic effects, they are also used medically as cough suppressants and antidiarrhoea agents. Opium itself is extracted from the opium poppy as a milky juice which is scraped off and left in a shaded area to dry and harden. One of its principal alkaloids is morphine, which is ten times more powerful than opium weight for weight, and is used medically for its analgesic qualities. Heroin is produced by boiling equal amounts of morphine with acetic anhydride, a colourless heavy liquid used in the manufacture of synthetic fibres and celluloid film. This combination is known as heroin base. Following several stages of production, including the addition of hydrochloric acid, strychnine and caffeine, as well as drying and sieving, heroin is produced. In its purest form, heroin is three or four times more powerful than morphine. Another alkaloid of opium is codeine, commonly used to treat coughs or as a mild analgesic. Codeine is about one-sixth the strength of morphine and its value at street level is not great.

Synthetic derivatives of the opiates mimic their action but are largely made from other materials. These include pethidine, dipinanone (Diconal), dextropropoxyphene (Distalgesic) and methadone (Physeptone). Pethidine is a short-acting analgesic and is often used for its postoperative effects. Diconal comes in tablet form and has proved to be popular in the illicit drug market as it contains an antinausea drug (cyclizine hydrochloride). Because it is not available in an injectable form, it has been liberally prescribed – but if the user does inject it, the consequences are disastrous, since it contains chalk and silicon.

Methadone is a synthetic drug which is often the drug of choice in the treatment of the opiate withdrawal syndrome. Traditionally methadone maintenance was considered to be the key to successful treatment, and reduction would take place only if or when the patient had become more stable. However, the view is now generally held within the treatment services that methadone is best used in the treatment of the physical withdrawal syndrome. Over 70% of addicts attending London clinics received oral methadone in 1984, compared to 29% in 1977 (Galton 1985).

An evaluation of heroin maintenance in a controlled trial randomly allocated 96 heroin addicts to treatment with injectable heroin or oral methadone (Hartnoll *et al.* 1980). It was found that heroin often maintained the status quo, whilst refusal to prescribe heroin and instead offering oral methadone led to a more confrontational response and resulted in a higher abstinence rate, but also a greater dependence on illegal sources of drugs for those who continued to inject.

Methadone is less common in injectable form and is usually given as an oral preparation with the appearance of a yellowy-brown linctus or as a green mixture. Chloroform is added as this makes injection painful.

Historically, opium smoking was first described amongst the Chinese. Until the seventeenth century it was primarily used as a medicine, but it gradually became popular as a commodity for barter in trading. In Europe opium was scrutinised for its medicinal purposes, and in 1805 Friedrich Sertürner isolated morphine from opium. By 1825, morphine was being marketed as a cure for opium addiction. Some physicians began to note with concern the addictive qualities of morphine; by 1874 heroin had been developed and was being marketed as a safe, non-addictive substitute for morphine. In the latter part of the nineteenth century, the Chinese in Britain became the focus of public attention and ire, as they were associated with the practice of opium smoking (Tyrer 1986).

Use in the twentieth century: at the beginning of the twentieth century, a series of meetings was held in an attempt to establish international narcotics legislation. Initially, attention focused on opium smuggling to the Far East. Developments were limited until the onset of World War I, and by 1917 the Defence of the Realm Act placed restrictions upon alcohol, opium and other psychotropic drugs. The majority of these drugs became restricted to medical prescribing. The 1920 Dangerous Drug Act widened the net of restrictions to include medical opium and morphine. Tensions increased between the Home Office and the Ministry of Health, highlighted by the views in the United States, where the prohibition movement was gaining momentum. The continued questioning of the right of doctors to prescribe for the purpose of medical treatment led to the setting up in 1924 of the Rolleston Committee to advise on the circumstances when (or if) morphine and heroin could be prescribed, and the precautions that should be taken in order to avoid abuse. The committee reported in 1926, and concluded that addiction to morphine and heroin was a rare occurrence and primarily occurred amongst medical professionals who had access to the drug. They laid down guidelines as to when it would be appropriate to prescribe heroin or morphine to addicts thus: (a) as part of a withdrawal regimen; (b) when the drug could not be withdrawn completely; (c) when it was apparent that the patient could not lead a normal life in the absence of such prescribing. This represented a major split for many years from the American approach.

In 1960, the Brain Committee reviewed the advice of Rolleston and stated that there had not been any significant changes since then. At that time, the need for any specialised units to assist the process of management and rehabilitation was not seen as important. By 1964, there had been a considerable rise in the number of people known to be addicted. In 1959 it was 454, but by 1964 it had risen to 753. In addition, a major difference was the emergence of users who were younger and did not have a medical background. The Brain Committee therefore produced a second report in 1965, and stated that the main reason for such a dramatic increase was overenthusiastic prescribing by a small number of doctors. Because so much was being dispensed, addicts were using the surplus to sell to their friends, thereby creating more and more addicts. The second report proposed that only a limited number of authorised doctors should be allowed to prescribe heroin and that prescription should take place in the context of rehabilitation. No authorisation was granted to doctors prescribing outside hospitals (general practitioners), and all doctors given licences were psychiatrists. As a result of acceptance of the proposal, 14 treatment centres were set up in London and 11 in the provinces. Thus, as well as providing medical treatment for the addicts, the role of the clinics was to restrict the availability of heroin and prevent an increase in the trend of use.

As the drug clinics were set up a system of notification was introduced, which required any doctor attending a person whom he or she suspected of addiction to certain controlled drugs to provide details to the Chief Medical Officer at the Home Office (Fig.2.1).

In the conclusions of their report, the Brain Committee stated the dilemma that faced the clinics:

> 'If there is insufficient control it may lead to the spread of addiction – as is happening at the present time. If on the other hand, the restrictions are so severe as to prevent or seriously discourage the addict from obtaining any supplies from legitimate sources, it may lead to the development of an organised illicit traffic. The absence hitherto of such an organised illicit traffic has been attributed largely to the fact that an addict has been able to obtain supplies legally. But this facility has now been abused with the result that addiction has increased.' (Brain Committee 1965)

Notification of addicts

The Misuse of Drugs (Notification of and Supply to Addicts) Regulations 1973 require that any doctor who attends a person who the doctor considers or has reasonable grounds to suspect, is addicted to any drug shall, within seven days of the attendance, furnish in writing particulars of that person to:

Chief Medical Officer
Home Office
Drugs Branch
Queen Anne's Gate
London SW1H 9AT

The drugs commonly in use to which the Regulations apply are:

Cocaine	Methadone
Dextromoramide	Morphine
Diamorphine	Opium
Dipipanone	Oxycodone
Hydrocodone	Pethidine
Hydromorphone	Phenazocine
Levorphanol	Piritramide

Note: A doctor may not prescribe, administer or supply cocaine, diamorphine or dipipanone for addiction without the necessary licence issued by the Home Secretary.

Particulars to be notified to the Chief Medical Officer are:

Name and address
Sex
Date of birth
National Health Service number
Date of attendance
Name of drug(s) of addiction

A new notification form for use by all notifying doctors was introduced on 1 September 1987. Notification must be confirmed annually in writing if the patient is still being treated by the practitioner. Notified information is incorporated in an Index of Addicts which is maintained in the Home Office and information from this is available on a confidential basis to doctors: in fact, it is good medical practice to check all new cases of addiction or suspected addiction with the Index before prescribing or supplying controlled drugs since this is a safeguard against addicts obtaining supplies simultaneously from two or more doctors. Enquiries can be made either in writing to the Chief Medical Officer or, preferably, by telephoning 01 273 2213. To keep notified information confidential, such enquiries are normally answered by means of a return telephone call. The reply will come from lay staff who are not qualified to give guidance on the clinical handling of cases. A recorded answering service is available for use by doctors out of office hours.

The preceding paragraph applies only to medical practitioners in England, Scotland and Wales. In Northern Ireland notification should be sent to the Chief Medical Officer, Department of Health and Social Services, Dundonald House, Belfast BT4 3SF, and any enquiries about the Northern Ireland Regulations or addicts should be made to that Department also at Dundonald House, telephone number 0232 650111 extension 229.

Figure 2.1   *Information on notification of addicts*

Recent pattern of use and cost: the early 1970s witnessed a relatively slow growth in the incidence and prevalence of heroin addiction. Supplies that were illegally imported from Southeast Asia via Hong Kong or Thailand became a major source of black market heroin, especially as supplies became scarce from legitimate prescribing. Police activity and a later series of bad harvests appeared to have temporarily limited supply and prices rose steadily until 1977/8. By then the retail price had risen to £75 per gram. As supplies from Southeast Asia diminished, Iranian heroin became in demand, and its influx grew as the Shah's empire fell and refugees needed easy ways of transferring their money and property into a transportable commodity (heroin). Since 1981, Pakistan and Afghanistan have become the primary source of supplies. The current price of illicitly imported heroin in London is £80 to £100 per gram. Relative to inflation, the price has fallen since 1978. Hartnoll *et al.* (1984) identified the following as factors in the recent growth of heroin use in Britain:

1   Increased availability of heroin of high purity and lower cost.
2   The change in route of administration, especially as sniffing became more popular.
3   The breakdown of many of the subcultural supports and taboos surrounding particular patterns of drug use in the late 1960s and early 1970s left a large population of people with experience of drug use.
4   Heroin became more cost-attractive relative to cannabis.
5   Dealers switched to selling a variety of drugs including heroin.

One source of information on the size of the heroin problem is the information collected by the Home Office, i.e. the notification scheme. It is generally accepted that the number of people using opioids on a heavy and regular basis is several times the number notified to the Home Office. However, generally the trend has been towards an increase in the number of notifications, with the figure for 1986 of drug addicts notified to the Home Office being 14 768.

During the 1960s heroin use was predominantly a phenomenon of adolescence or early adulthood. By the early 1980s users were more likely to be in their mid to late twenties to thirties. Over the past few years, younger people have become increasingly involved. Also, the proportion of females has increased to 30%.

In the early 1970s about half the heavy opiate users in Britain were seen and notified, but over the past few years as the use of the drug has increased, the proportion in treatment has fallen. It is suggested that the total number of people in the United Kingdom who used opiates regularly during 1985 was somewhere between 60 000 and 80 000 (Hartnoll 1986).

Hartnoll *et al.* (1986) in their handbook *Assessing local drug problems: a short guide* state that because drug use is both illegal and stigmatised, two important issues are raised: (a) drug use is not easily assessed through normal health or social service channels, and (b) if no specialised services exist and if the level of knowledge or expertise is minimal, then there is no easy and quick way of conducting an assessment. They suggest that the combination of figures from several sources may help to assess the nature and extent of the problem:

1. *Routine statistics* – Home Office notifications; police statistics (seizures of controlled drugs and arrests involving controlled drugs); drug-related mortalities; hospital inpatient statistics; hepatitis statistics; prescription of psychoactive drugs.
2. *Information obtained from the following agencies* – drug treatment centres; general practitioners; accident and emergency departments; coroners; police; probation officers; etc.
3. *Information obtained from groups and individuals in the local community* – drug users; self-help groups; community/tenant associations; local media.

Legal status: opioids are controlled under the Misuse of Drugs Act which makes it illegal to supply or possess them without a prescription. It is also illegal to produce, import or export them without authority. It is an offence to allow premises to be used for producing or supplying these drugs. Restrictions allow only specially licensed doctors to prescribe heroin or cocaine for anything other than a physical illness.

Route of administration: opioid powders can be swallowed or dissolved in water and injected. Heroin is rarely swallowed but can be sniffed or smoked. When smoked, heroin powder is heated and the fumes inhaled, a practice known as 'chasing' or 'chasing the dragon'. Opium itself is either eaten or smoked. Some opioid mixtures are rendered non-injectable by the addition of substances used to dissolve the powder.

Effects: the short-term effects of opiates vary depending upon the route of administration. If the drug is taken intravenously the effects are virtually instantaneous and short-lived. Intramuscular injection produces a slower and less intense effect, somewhat similar to the effect caused by sniffing. The effects following smoking are relatively quick, but are much less intense. Opioids in moderate doses, in addition to their analgesic qualities, produce a range of mild physical effects. They depress the CNS and thereby affect coughing, respiration and heart rate. Dilation of the blood vessels produces a feeling of warmth, and depression of bowel motility may lead to constipation. At higher doses, the user becomes sedated and appears drowsy and contented. If the dose is increased further, stupor and coma are likely to occur. Death is unlikely from respiratory failure, although the risk is greatly increased by a high dose of the opiate and the presence of other depressant drugs (e.g. alcohol).

Reports about the experiences following first use of opiates vary. A common experience appears to be drowsiness, a sense of well-being, warmth and contentment. These sensations are often described as the 'rush', and relate to the warm feeling in the stomach which flows throughout the body, producing an overall calm, especially following intravenous administration. Feelings of detachment from pain and anxiety are often associated with desires for food and sex. As well as the pleasurable effects, a common experience is nausea and vomiting. For some people this may act as a deterrent, but for others more of the drug is used to retain the feeling of euphoria.

Regular use of opiates leads to tolerance, and the user requires increased doses to produce the necessary effects. As well as seeking greater amounts of the drug, the user may change the method of administration, using the intravenous route for a more intense and immediate experience. Physical dependence occurs as the body adapts to the presence of the drug and withdrawal symptoms occur if its use is stopped abruptly.

Withdrawal from opiates may occur as early as a few hours after the last administration. The symptoms are often comparable to a bout of influenza and include uneasiness, yawning, tears, diarrhoea and abdominal cramps. These symptoms are accompanied by a craving for the drug and they peak between 48 hours and 72 hours after the last dose. The syndrome subsides after about a week, although it takes several months for bodily functions to return to normal.

The immediate physical consequences of long-term opioid use are rarely serious in themselves. However, serious physical problems are often a result of injecting opioids and the drug-orientated lifestyle and subculture. Poor hygiene and the use of adulterants result in infections associated with unsterile injection techniques, e.g. tetanus, abscesses and cellulitis. Pulmonary complications, including various types of pneumonia, may also result from the lifestyle and the depressant effects of opiates on respiration. As the drug user loses his or her appetite and becomes more apathetic, the risk of self-neglect and illness increases.

Difficulties are experienced by opiate dependent women during pregnancy and childbirth. There is a much higher incidence of spontaneous abortion and premature birth. The newborn babies of addicted mothers often develop a withdrawal syndrome and exhibit sneezing, extreme restlessness, shrill crying, tremor tachycardia, fluid loss from sweating, polyuria, diarrhoea, fever and generalised cramps (Stauber *et al.* 1982).

Approximately 8% of drug users have a positive Australia antigen test and are either carriers or are incubating hepatitis B. Hepatitis B is spread via body fluids, so that kissing, sexual intercourse and the use of unsterile needles for injecting or tattooing are the probable routes of infection. In about one in every thousand cases acute hepatitis B develops into acute hepatic failure.

AIDS AND HIV INFECTION

AIDS (acquired immune deficiency syndrome) is a condition where the body's immune system breaks down, leaving it vulnerable to infections and rare cancers which would not normally affect healthy people.

The causative agent in AIDS is a retrovirus now known as HIV (human immunodeficiency virus). The virus is found in body fluids, particularly blood and semen, and is transmitted in similar ways to hepatitis B virus:

> through exchange of body fluids, especially during penetrative sexual intercourse
> through sharing injection equipment (needles, syringes, spoons) contaminated with infected blood
> from an infected mother to her unborn child (probably via the placenta).

Once infected with HIV an individual *remains* infected and potentially infectious to others via these routes of transmission.

Injecting drug users, their sexual partners and their unborn children are thus particularly at risk from HIV infection and AIDS. Unlike the case with hepatitis B virus, there appears to be no natural immunity in individuals to HIV and there is at present no vaccine to confer immunity. In addition, pregnancy appears to trigger the development of fullblown AIDS in infected mothers. Women are thus at double risk of giving birth to infected babies and going on to develop AIDS in the process.

Currently available HIV antibody tests, performed on blood samples, do not detect the presence of live virus and do not indicate whether an infected individual will go on to develop AIDS. Their use in screening drug users has therefore only a limited value and would appear to work best in the context of individual counselling, health education and drug treatment programmes (Buning *et al.* 1986, Des Jarlais *et al.* 1985). Most are agreed, however, that women who have shared 'works' or who are the partners of men with a history of injecting drug use in the past six years should seriously consider the test if they are planning to have children.

Once HIV is established in the drug-using community, the spread of the virus both through it and beyond can be swift and alarming (Des Jarlais 1986, Robertson *et al.* 1986). Because there is as yet no known vaccine for HIV and no known cure for AIDS most agencies have concentrated on preventative strategies, which have included:

> health education about AIDS and advice on risk-education behaviour (using sterile needles, condoms, etc.)
> providing sterile injection equipment to users to prevent the need to share
> provision of increased treatment facilities for drug users, including oral drug substitutes to get people away from injecting.

A willingness to provide various combinations of these strategies would appear to be more effective than a blanket policy, since the needs of drug users, and their patterns of behaviour, will often be specifically related to local drug scenes (e.g. both New York and Edinburgh have high rates of HIV infection amongst their drug users but the approaches to the problem in both cities have been very different – Edinburgh has no equivalent of the street scene in New York where it is, for example, an offence merely to possess a needle and syringe).

REFERENCES

Balter M. D., Levine J., Manheim M. A. (1974). Cross-national study of the extent of anti-anxiety/sedative drug use. *New England Journal of Medicine*, 290, 769–74.

Brain Committee (1960). *Report of the Inter-departmental Committee on Drug Addiction*. London: HMSO.

Brain Committee (1965). *Report of the Inter-departmental Committee on Drug Addiction*. London: HMSO.

Buning E. C., Coutinho R. A., Van Brussell G. H. A., *et al.* (1986). Preventing AIDS in drug addicts in Amsterdam. *Lancet*, 1, 1435.

Committee On The Review of Medicines (1979). Recommendations on barbiturate preparations. *British Medical Journal*, 2, 719–20.

Des Jarlais D. C. (1986). *HTLV-III/LAV-Associated Disease Progression and Co-Factors in a Cohort of New York IV Drug Abusers*. Communication 197 Second International Conference on AIDS, Paris, June 23–25.

Des Jarlais D. C., Friedman S. R., Hopkins W. (1985). Risk reduction for the acquired immune deficiency syndrome among intravenous drug users. *Annals of Internal Medicine*, 103, 755.

Fornazzi L., Wilkinson D. A., Kapur B. M., et al. (1983). Cerebellar, cortical and functional impairment in toluene abusers. *Acta Neurologica Scandinavica*, 67, 319–29.

Galton, I. (1985). A review of prescribing practices amongst London drug dependence clinics 1977–84. Unpublished, Middlesex Polytechnic.

Gossop M. (1982). *Living with Drugs*. London: Temple Smith.

Hartnoll R. L., Lewis R., Bryer S. (1984). Recent trends in drug use in Britain. *Druglink*, 19, 22–4.

Hartnoll R. L. (1980). Evaluation of heroin maintenance in controlled trial. *Archives of General Psychiatry*, 37, 877–84.

Hartnoll R. L. (1986). Recent trends in drug use in Britain. *Druglink*, 1 (2), 12–14.

Herzderg J. L., Wolkind S. N. (1983). Solvent sniffing in perspective. *British Journal of Hospital Medicine*, 29, 72–6.

Hofmann A. (1980). *LSD: My Problem Child*. New York: McGraw-Hill.

Hortwitz J. A. (1977). The pathways into psychiatric treatment: some differences between men and women. *Journal of Health Social Behaviour*, 18, 169–72.

Institute for the Study of Drug Dependence (1985). *Drug Abuse Briefing*. London: ISDD.

Institute for the Study of Drug Dependence (1986). *Surveys and Statistics on Drug Taking in Britain*. London: ISDD.

Jamieson A., Glanz A., MacGregor S. (1984). *Dealing with Drug Misuse – Crisis Intervention in the City*. London: Tavistock.

Kramer J. F., Cameron D. C. (1975). *A Manual On Drug Dependence*. Geneva: WHO.

Lader M., (1978). Benzodiazepines – the opium of the masses, *Neuroscience*, 3, 159–65.

Marks J. (1983). The benzodiazepines – for good or evil. *Neuropsychobiology*, 10, 115–26.

Ministry of Health and Scottish Home and Health Department (1965). *Drug Addiction*. The Second Report of the Interdepartmental Committee: HMSO.

Murphy S. M., Owen R. T., Tyrer P. J. (1984). Withdrawal symptoms after six weeks treatment with diazepam. *Lancet*, ii, 1389.

National Institute on Drug Abuse. (1984). *Cocaine: Pharmacology, Effects and Treatment of Abuse*. Rockville, USA: DHHS Publications.

Parish P. (1971). The prescribing of psychotropic drugs in general practice. *Journal of the Royal College of General Practitioners*, 21 (4), 1–77.

Parry H. J., Balter M. B., Mellinger G. D., Cisin I. H., Manheimer D. I. (1973). National patterns of psychotherapeutic drug use. *Archives of General Psychiatry*, 7 (28), 769–83.

Petursson H., Lader M. (1984). *Dependence on Tranquillizers*. Oxford: OUP.

Robertson J. R., Bucknall A. B. V., Welsby P. D., et al. (1986). Epidemic of AIDS related virus (HTLV III/LAV) infection among intravenous drug abusers. *British Medical Journal*, 292, 527.

Rogers H. (1982). Glue sniffing among schoolchildren. *Health Visitor Journal*, 55, 236–9.

Ron M. A. (1986). Volatile substance abuse: a review of possible long-term neurological intellectual and psychiatric sequelae. *British Journal of Psychiatry*, **148**, 235–46.

Sansum G. (1984). Glue sniffing – a study. *Nursing Times*, 714–15.

Skegg D. C. G., Doll R., Perry J. (1977). Use of medicines in general practice. *British Medical Journal*, 1, 1561–3.

Stauber M., Schwerdt M., Tylden E. (1982). Pregnancy, birth and puerperium in women suffering from heroin addiction. *Journal of Psychosomatic Obstetrics and Gynaecology*, 1–3'4, 128–38.

Tyler A. (1984). *Street Drugs*. London: New English Library.

Tyrer P., Rutherford D., Huggett A. (1981). Benzodiazepine withdrawal symptoms and propranolol. *Lancet*, i, 520–2.

Watson J. (1979). Glue sniffing. *British Medicine*, 7 November, 31–3.

Williams P. (1981). Trends in the prescribing of psychotropic drugs. In *The Misuse of Psychotropic Drugs* (Murry R., Ghodlse H., Harris C., Williams D., Williams P., eds). London: Gaskell Invicta Press, pp. 7–12.

Wootton Committee (1968). Report by the advisory committee on drug dependency. London: HMSO.

World Health Organisation. (1952). Technical Report Series No.48. Geneva: WHO.

Chapter 3

The effects of alcohol

In most societies (with the main exception of Moslem societies) ethyl alcohol is generally accepted as a legal psychotropic drug for adult use. Alcohol is easily produced by the process of fermentation and has probably played a part in the development of human civilisation for at least 5000 years. Its uses have varied from medicinal anaesthetic to being an adjunct of religious ceremonies, but it is primarily a drug used to enhance social intercourse.

What is alcohol?

The chemical formula of ethyl alcohol or ethanol is C_2H_5OH – it is therefore a molecule consisting of carbon, hydrogen and oxygen. During fermentation, yeast utilises sugar, water and air to produce ethanol and carbon dioxide. As the yeast builds up higher concentrations of ethanol, it becomes more and more intoxicated by its own product, until at about 13% to 15% the yeast ceases to ferment. It is by this process that beverages are produced such as lagers, beers (all strengths), ciders and table wines. Specific alcoholic drinks are produced during fermentation by the use of different substrates – e.g. beer from hops, lager from barley and wine from grapes.

In order to produce stronger beverages, distillation is required. This process involves boiling off the ethanol from the sugar and water and cooling and condensing the alcohol vapour, so that the concentrated spirit can be collected. It would be impossible to produce 'pure' alcohol of 100% content. The strength of alcoholic beverages can be theoretically expressed as the volume of alcohol in the drink as a percentage of the total volume of the drink (see Table 3.1). The higher the alcohol content, the less the beverage will contain elements other than alcohol and water. Whilst beers and wines contain small amounts of minerals, distilled spirits contain virtually only alcohol and water. Because there are considerable differences in the strengths of beer and wine compared to distilled spirits, it is sometimes assumed that the

Table 3.1 *Alcohol content by volume of alcoholic drinks*

Drink	Alcohol content (%)
Beers and lagers	2–5
Strong beers and lagers	6–10
Cider	5–12
Table wines	6–15
Sparkling wines	15–17
Fortified wines (e.g. sherry, port, vermouth)	17–20
Liqueurs	30–55
Spirits	37–40

beers and wines are safer than spirits. However, because of the much greater total volume of a glass of beer compared with a tot of whisky, a half pint of ordinary beer contains virtually the same amount of alcohol as the measure of whisky. As a means of developing a common measure of alcohol consumption irrespective of the specific beverage, the term unit of alcohol is commonly used (Table 3.2).

Table 3.2 *Units of alcohol in various beverages (London Weekend Television 1985)*

	Quantity	Units
Beer and lager		
Ordinary strength beer or lager	½ pint	1
	1 pint	2
	1 can	1½
Export beer	1 pint	2½
	1 can	2
Strong ale or lager	½ pint	2½
	1 pint	4
	1 can	3
Extra strength beer or lager	½ pint	2½
	1 pint	5
	1 can	4
Cider		
Average cider	½ pint	1½
	1 pint	3
	quart bottle	6
Strong cider	½ pint	2
	1 pint	4
	quart bottle	8

Table 3.2 *Continued*

	Quantity	Units
Spirits	1 standard	
	pub measure	1
	1 bottle	30
Table wine	1 standard glass	1
	1 bottle (70 cl)	7
	1 litre bottle	10
Sherry and fortified wine	1 standard	
	pub measure	1
	1 bottle	12

In addition to alcohol and water, substances called 'congeners' are added to the drink which give it a particular look, flavour, smell and taste. These include vegetable products, various chemicals and minute amounts of metal and other constituents derived from the recipes of the beverage and/or the apparatus in which it is brewed or distilled. They are strongly associated with the unpleasant symptoms of hangover: the greater the amount of congeners – the more severe the hangover! Beverages that contain small amounts of congeners include vodka, gin and white wine; brandies, ports and red wines contain large amounts of congeners (Fig.3.1).

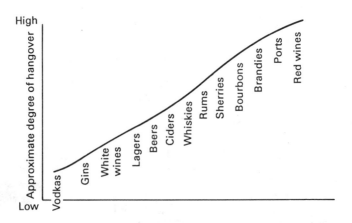

Figure 3.1   *Amount of congeners in various unmixed beverages (Plant 1982)*

Absorption and metabolism

Almost all the alcohol from beverages passes unchanged into the bloodstream. About 95% is oxidised by the liver and 5% is excreted unchanged in the urine, sweat and breath. Most alcohol is absorbed through the duodenum and ileum rather than the stomach. However, the stomach reacts to strong drinks by closing the pyloric sphincter and thereby delaying the absorption of alcohol. Food and the protective mucus from the stomach lining also play a part in the delay of absorption.

Low-strength drinks are not sufficiently concentrated to diffuse through the stomach wall and therefore their absorption is slow.

Enzymes assist in the absorption of alcohol across the walls of the intestine and through this process alcohol is transported from the intestinal system to the circulatory system. There is evidence that women absorb alcohol faster than men and therefore reach peak blood alcohol concentrations faster. Another difference is that women have about 50% of their body weight in the form of water, whereas for men it is about 60%. As alcohol is concentrated in this area, women will show higher blood alcohol concentrations and therefore are likely to experience greater complications than a man of the same size who drinks the same amount. The portal system takes the alcohol to the liver where the alcohol is broken down and oxidised by the enzyme alcohol dehydrogenase (Fig.3.2). This produces acetaldehyde which in turn is converted into acetic acid by the enzyme acetaldehyde dehydrogenase. The acetic acid is quickly turned into carbon dioxide and water with a major release of energy.

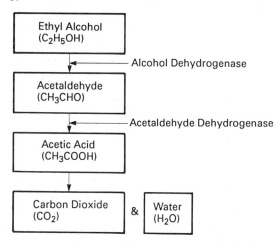

Figure 3.2 *The metabolism of alcohol*

There are several by-products of the metabolism of alcohol. Lactic acid is produced in large quantities, and may play a part in the incidence amongst many heavy drinkers of feelings of panic and anxiety. Uric acid is present in increased amounts in the blood of heavy drinkers and is associated with gout and arthritis.

Breakdown and excretion

As alcohol in the blood circulates around the body, most of it returns to the liver to be converted to acetaldehyde and gradually broken down and diluted. Irrespective of the amount of alcohol present in the body, the liver retains a rate of breakdown of approximately one unit per hour.

Terminology

There has been over the past few years a move to replace the term 'alcoholic' with terms such as 'problem drinkers' and 'alcohol-related problems'. The word 'alcoholic' was first coined by Huss in the late 1840s and the condition was regarded as a disease (Huss 1849). Being an alcoholic also had connotations of low morals and brought upon the person the general wrath of society.

Jellinek (1960) described addiction to alcohol as being a specific diagnostic category, and his elaboration of the natural history or developmental course of the addiction process exemplified the disease model. Most world authorities retained elements of the disease model, and the World Health Organisation's definition (1952) read in part:

'Alcoholics are those excessive drinkers where dependence on alcohol has attained such a degree that it shows a noticeable mental disturbance or an interference with their bodily and mental health.'

Keller's definition (1960) also refers to the disease model:

'Alcoholism is a chronic disease manifested by repeated implicative drinking so as to cause injury to the drinker's health or to his social or economic functioning.'

The disease model had certain advantages; it removed some of the moral connotations and helped a shift from punitive measures to the provisions of medical and psychological treatment. There are also distinct disadvantages: overemphasis of the disease model leads to the erroneous assumption that alcoholism is a single entity, similar to tuberculosis or diabetes. The model perpetuates the doctor–patient relationship, encouraging the patient to maintain a passive role. It can also have the effect of creating a self-fulfilling prophecy ('once an alcoholic, always an alcoholic'); early problem drinkers may be frightened away from treatment by such catchphrases.

It is becoming clearer that there is in the population a range of people who use alcohol to cope with difficulties and that the aetiology of alcohol problems is complex. A useful definition is that of Plaut (1969), who said:

> 'An individual who (1) responds to beverage alcohol in a certain way, perhaps physiologically determined by experiencing relief and relaxation, and (2) has certain personality characteristics such as difficulty in dealing with and overcoming depression, frustration and anxiety, and who (3) is a member of a culture in which there is both pressure to drink and culturally induced guilt and confusion regarding what kind of drinking behaviour is appropriate, is more likely to develop trouble than most people.'

Heather and Robinson (1986) also question the disease model and suggest that problem drinking is a learned habitual behaviour; they say:

> 'We should stop trying to ignore alcohol problems by putting the blame for them on individual alcoholics, as is the disease model view. Instead, we should make them a matter of collective responsibility in which the whole of society is involved.'

Edwards (1982) describes the following as the elements of the alcohol dependence syndrome:

1 Narrowing of drinking repertoire – the person becomes less adaptable in choosing when to drink and when to abstain or to be moderate.
2 Salience of drinking – a preoccupation with alcohol dominates the person's life.
3 Increased tolerance to alcohol – the person can maintain activities with an intake that would render light drinkers incapable.
4 Repeated withdrawal symptoms.
5 Relief drinking to avoid withdrawal symptoms.
6 Subjective awareness of compulsion to drink.
7 Tendency for harmful pattern of drinking to recur after periods of abstinence.

However, such specific criteria need to be viewed with caution as it is likely that they will identify only a small group of people, whereas there are many more who have a problem associated with the misuse of alcohol. In 1977, the Advisory Committee on Alcoholism reported:

> 'Surveys based on different definitions, using different survey techniques, have produced different results of the number of problem drinkers.' (DHSS 1977)

Patterns of consumption

Most people who drink alcohol enjoy it and do not suffer serious problems as a result. Arguably, it can be said that the consumption of alcohol plays a crucial role in aiding social intercourse. By tradition Britain has been a beer-drinking country and it was often considered safer in the past to drink beer rather than water. In the 1680s consumption reached a peak of 2 to 3 pints per person per day, about four times the present figure (Spring and Buss 1977). During the eighteenth century, gin rather than poverty was often presented as the cause of such evils as the high infant mortality rate. In 1751 and 1752 legislation was passed which restricted the availability of spirits and therefore reduced consumption. At various times in the nineteenth century, legislation was introduced to curb the consumption of alcohol, and towards the end of the century per capita consumption was greatly decreased, although it was about 10% above that of today.

During the First World War restrictions and controls on alcohol consumption were instituted, which ensured that the pattern of reduced per capita consumption was maintained for the first half of the twentieth century. Between the early 1930s and the early 1950s, per capita alcohol intake in the form of spirits was kept at a level almost one-sixth of the 1900 figure.

Figure 3.3 illustrates the overall changes in total per capita consumption and the per capita consumption for beer, spirits and wine. Wine sales are four times higher than the 1900 level and are higher than at any time in the past. Beer drinking has fluctuated during the twentieth century and has now returned to 1900 levels.

Cost and availability

In the United Kingdom, alcohol has become cheaper in real terms. The time taken in minutes to earn the cost of a bottle of whisky by a manual worker on average pay in the years since 1945 is shown in Table 3.3.

Table 3.3. *Minutes worked by manual worker on average pay to earn the cost of a bottle of whisky or a pint of beer* (Rutherford 1988).

	1945	1950	1970	1976	1988
Whisky	673	659	235	209	115
Beer	27	23	11.4	12	8.34

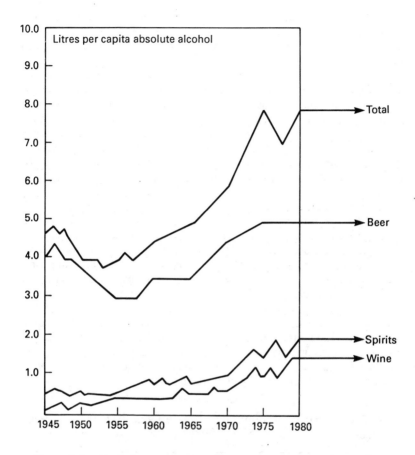

Figure 3.3 *Alcohol consumption by type in the United Kingdom 1945–79 (Office of Health Economics)*

There has also been a major increase in the number of retail outlets in the United Kingdom. The 1961 Licensing Act and the abolition of resale price maintenance in 1966/7 encouraged supermarkets and grocers to sell alcohol. The purchase of alcohol especially by women has become a norm such that it is integrated in the weekly shopping with the beans and baby food.

Current drinking habits

Much research has focused upon the level of alcohol consumption in the United Kingdom. Some researchers have examined a relatively small geographical area (Edwards *et al.* 1972), whilst there have been national surveys and a special project completed by the Office of Population Censuses and Surveys (Wilson 1980). Dight (1976) has completed an investigation of Scottish drinking habits. Most of these studies show the highest consumption among young, unmarried, separated or divorced males. Dight found that 30% of all Scottish drinking was reported by only 3% of the population; many of these were single men in their late teens or early twenties. Female drinking has increased, and amongst the many factors associated with it are the change in society's attitude to women drinking and the greater access to alcohol via supermarkets.

Recent OPCS data on UK drinking levels, measured in units and related to age and sex, are shown in Tables 3.4 and 3.5. When the consumption during the last week by sex is examined, there is evidence that in England, Scotland and Wales 6% of men over 20 and 11% of women do not drink at all. However, in Northern Ireland, almost a third of men and half of all women are teetotal. This information suggests that despite a similar per capita consumption, very different drinking styles occur in different countries (Table 3.6), and this has considerable implications for the management of people with alcohol problems. The Scottish or Irish drinking man who generally drinks greater amounts on fewer days may experience more acute physical and legal problems than his English counterpart, whose consumption is often more evenly spread throughout the week.

Table 3.4 *Average consumption in standard units of those who drank last week, by age and sex* (Office of Population Censuses and Surveys).

Age	Men (%)			Women (%)		
	England & Wales	Scotland	N. Ireland	England & Wales	Scotland	N. Ireland
20 – 27	26.6	26.2	18.9	9.7	7.7	7.0
28 – 37	19.7	24.9	15.2	6.4	6.3	6.9
38 – 47	19.5	20.9	14.4	7.7	6.2	
48 – 57	20.1	16.1	12.3	7.2	6.1	5.4
58 – 67	15.5	13.5	9.9	4.4	3.9	
68 +	11.7	6.4		5.0		
all aged 20+	19.6	19.5	14.5	7.0	6.2	6.5

Table 3.5 *Consumption in preceding week by sex* (Office of Population Censuses and Surveys).

	Men aged 20 or over (%)			Women aged 20 or over (%)		
	England & Wales	Scotland	N. Ireland	England & Wales	Scotland	N. Ireland
Nothing (and nothing in the last year, i.e. teetotal)	6.0	7.0	31.0	11.0	11.0	53.0
Nothing (but had had a drink in the last year)	18.0	15.0	23.0	32.0	34.0	27.0
1–5 units	20.0	21.0	14.0	34.0	33.0	14.0
6–10 units	14.0	12.0	11.0	10.0	13.0	3.0
11–20 units	16.0	18.0	12.0	10.0	7.0	1.0
21–35 units	13.0	14.0	5.0	2.0	3.0	1.0
36–50 units	8.0	8.0	1.0			
51 units or more	6.0	6.0	3.0	1.0	0.0	1.0
Average consumption of drinkers in preceding week	19.6	19.5	14.5	7.0	6.2	6.5

Table 3.6 *Proportion of abstainers in the countries of Europe* (Davies and Walsh 1983).

Country	Percentage Abstainers
Ireland	43
Poland	19
Austria	17
Norway	15
Sweden	13
Switzerland	11
UK	
England & Wales	9
Scotland	9
Northern Ireland	34
Netherlands	< 10
West Germany	5–10
Belgium	< 5
Denmark	< 5
Luxembourg	1.5
Italy	< 1
France	< 1
Spain	No data

The extent of the problem

In order to assess the extent of the alcohol problem, some consensus needs to be reached about what are considered to be sensible levels of alcohol consumption. To use the term 'safe' amount is not ideal, for there may be occasions when the safe amount is zero. Consultations between the Health Education Authority, Alcohol Concern and representatives of the medical professions in 1986 have led to a new agreement about sensible drinking limits.

With the aim of simplifying the information to the public, the limits can be represented as three zones of low, moderate and high risk (Fig.3.4). Some people find it helpful to talk about these as green, amber and red areas.

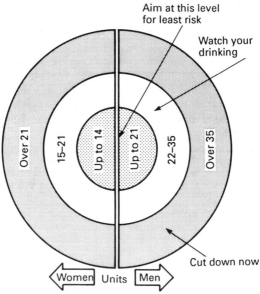

Figure 3.4 *Weekly drinking target*

Defining the extent of the problem in very specific terms creates many difficulties. Such indices as cirrhosis death rates or admission to psychiatric hospital with a diagnosis of alcoholism only provide a picture of a very small amount of people. In its paper '*Alcohol – reducing the harm*', the Office of Health Economics has attempted to put round figures on the problem (Table 3.7).

Table 3.7 *Number of heavy drinkers, problem drinkers and alcohol dependents – England and Wales 1970s (OHE 1981).*

	High estimate	Low estimate	OHE estimate
Heavy drinkers	3 000 000	1 300 000	3 000 000
Problem drinkers	1 300 000	500 000	700 000
Alcohol dependents	240 000	70 000	150 000

In overall terms, the OHE estimates indicate that about 8% of the total adult population are heavy drinkers, 2% are problem drinkers and 0.4% are alcohol dependent. Women are outnumbered by men on a 1:5 ratio, but it is possible that this relates to under-reporting by women of their consumption, due to the hostile views of society.

Immediate effects of drinking alcohol

Alcohol taken in small doses provides a sense of well-being and stimulates the digestive juices. If large amounts are taken in a short space of time, the drinker becomes inebriated. The immediate effect of alcohol is dependent upon the amount, the frequency, the mood and expectation of outcome after ingestion. Blood alcohol concentration (BAC) measures the amount of alcohol present in the bloodstream, and Table 3.8 describes the effect of alcohol at different BACs. A standard unit contains about 15 mg of alcohol.

Table 3.8 *BAC and Effects*

BAC (mg/100ml)	Effect
20	Moderate or light drinker experiences a feeling of relaxation and sense of well-being.
40	Feelings of well-being increased, association with mild disinhibition. Increased likelihood of accidents.
60	Impairment of judgement and foresight. Ability to make considered decision is affected.
80	Physical coordination diminishes; the legal limit for driving.
100	Drunkenness is perceived by an observer, continued deterioration in physical, psychological and social competence.
140	Drunkenness associated with staggering and double vision.
300	Loss of consciousness, but can be roused.
450–500	Breathing stops, leading to coma and death.

Longer-term effects of drinking alcohol

A useful way of encapsulating the effects of alcohol consumption is to examine it on three levels:

1　Problems related to intoxication.
2　Problems relating to regular, heavy alcohol consumption.
3　Problems relating to dependence.

Intoxication

The majority of drinkers will at some stage in their drinking careers experience problems associated with intoxication. The nature of such problems will vary from individual to individual, but could well include some of the following:

Medical problems – acute alcohol poisoning or overdose, amnesic episodes, acute gastritis, pancreatitis, trauma, head injury and accidents.

Social problems – social isolation, aggressive behaviour, domestic violence, child abuse or neglect, sexual problems, relationship problems, and work difficulties including accidents, absenteeism and poor timekeeping.

Legal problems – driving or drunkenness offences, theft, shoplifting and assault.

Psychological problems – depression and suicide attempts or gestures.

To highlight some of these problems, it is worth noting some recent research reports by Jeffs and Saunders (1983); they reported an investigation by one police force which found that 64% of all persons arrested had been drinking in the four hours prior to their arrest, and that between the hours of 10 p.m. and 2 a.m. 93% of people arrested were intoxicated. It is notable that in the period 1952 to 1982, during which time alcohol consumption nearly doubled, convictions of drunkenness rose from 15.9 per 10 000 adults to 30.9 per 10 000 adults. A recent OPCS estimate is that 10% of male drinkers break the drinking and driving laws each week (Wilson 1980).

A similarly worrying pattern can be observed in studies of the social and medical problems. For example, alcohol intoxication has been implicated in the following:

1　80% of deaths from fire (Strathclyde Regional Council 1981)
2　two-thirds of parasuicides (Platt 1983)
3　62% of serious head injuries in males (Galbraith *et al.* 1976)
4　45% of fatal road traffic accidents involving young people (Harvard 1977)
5　one-third of all domestic accidents (Taylor 1981)
6　30% of non-traffic accident fatalities (Murray 1977)

7 30% of drownings (Royal Society for the Prevention of Accidents 1983).

Problems related to excessive use

From the perspective of medical problems, a study by Barrison (1982) suggested that between 15.6% and 23.2% of hospital admissions were abnormal drinkers. The important factor is that the regular, daily (or nearly daily) use of alcohol may lead to a high tolerance for alcohol, and such drinkers – although never appearing intoxicated – may over many years of regular use develop a wide variety of consequences. Certain occupations facilitate the regular use of alcohol; these include sales representatives, medicine, the armed forces, workers in the hotel and entertainment industry and those employed in the production and retail of alcoholic beverages.

For cirrhosis of the liver, publicans have a mortality rate fifteen times the average, fishermen six times and medical practitioners three times the average (Table 3.9).

Table 3.9 *Liver cirrhosis mortality, England and Wales 1970–1972* (OPCS 1978).

Occupation	Standard Mortality Rate
Publicans, innkeepers	1576
Deck officers, engineering officers, ships' pilots	781
Barmen, barmaids	633
Deck and engineroom ratings, barge and boatmen	628
Fishermen	595
Proprietors and managers in boarding houses and hotels	506
Finance brokers, insurance brokers, financial agents	392
Restaurateurs	385
Lorry drivers' mates, van guards	377
Armed forces (British and overseas)	367
Cooks	354
Shunters, pointsmen	323
Winders, reelers	319
Electrical engineers	319
Authors, journalists and related workers	314
Medical practitioners	311
Garage proprietors	294
Signalmen and railway-crossing keepers	290
Maids, valets and related service workers	281
Tobacco preparers and product makers	269
Metallurgists	266

Specific medical, social, legal and psychological problems are associated with regular excessive consumption of alcohol.

Medical problems – cancers of the mouth, throat and oesophagus, oesophageal varices, gastritis, stomach/duodenal ulcers, pancreatitis, vitamin deficiency, impotence, cardiomyopathy, peripheral neuropathy, liver problems (fatty liver → hepatitis → cirrhosis), epilepsy and fetal alcohol syndrome. As our alcohol consumption has increased over the past thirty years, so too have liver cirrhosis death rates, being in 1950 2.7 per 100 000 and by 1981 4.9 per 100 000. We should remember that liver cirrhosis represents the extreme end of the alcohol-related physical damage spectrum, and many of the other disorders mentioned above can create problems.

Social problems – financial debt, marital problems, family problems, work problems (absenteeism, demotion, unemployment) and sexual difficulties.

Legal problems – offences such as theft, deception and fraud.

Psychological problems – depression, phobias, anxiety, suicide risks and brain damage (Wernicke's encephalopathy, Korsakoff's psychosis).

The above list is an illustration of some of the many consequences of regular excessive consumption.

Problems relating to dependence

Included under this heading are those people who have traditionally been labelled 'alcoholics'. There are considerable difficulties with this terminology, and the World Health Organisation no longer uses the word. Most people medically diagnosed as having 'alcoholism' will experience problems of intoxication and problems of regular use, as well as problems of dependence. Dependence can be of a physical and/or psychological nature. The alcohol dependence syndrome, previously described by Edwards (1982), provides a useful framework of criteria for looking at the considerable number of clients who have moved beyond the stages of intoxication and regular excessive consumption. Such a syndrome is often associated with many sociocultural influences which may play a crucial role in ensuring the continuation of the behaviour. Dependence can be associated with many medical/psychological, social and legal problems.

Medical/psychological problems – anxiety, phobias, depression, hallucinations, withdrawal symptoms, delirium tremens, epilepsy and personality change.

Social problems – family problems, financial problems and work problems.

Legal problems – fraud, theft.

Withdrawal symptoms

When someone who is dependent on alcohol stops drinking, they will experience withdrawal symptoms, which can be mild or severe.

During the early withdrawal phase the following symptoms may be present: the smell of alcohol is often still evident; shakes or tremor nearly always evident up to 48 hours after cessation of drinking; anxiety and agitation; flushing of the skin, sweating; sleeplessness and restlessness; fits may occur during the first 48 hours, with a peak frequency between 13 and 18 hours; seizures can continue up to five days.

With alcoholic hallucinosis the following symptoms may be present: visual and auditory hallucinations but orientated to time, place and person; intense psychomotor agitation (e.g. easily startled, tremors, jerking movements); acute anxiety.

Delirium tremens – symptoms start suddenly and usually peak three days after the last drink; paranoia and disorientation to time, place and person (a key sign); intense restlessness; hallucinations; fever, tachycardia; profuse sweating; and any other signs from the phases indicated previously.

A vivid account of the personal experience of delirium tremens is recounted in 'The day the strangers came' (*Nursing Times* 1984). The author recalls, 'large black snakes reared their ugly heads and tried to bite me; little black spiders crawled all over the pillow and up the walls'.

Major conditions associated with alcohol misuse

To consider in any detail all the conditions associated with alcohol misuse could take several chapters. The following conditions are those with which nurses may come into regular contact.

Cancer

Most of the cancers are associated with the upper digestive tract, such as the tongue, mouth, pharynx, larynx, oesophagus. A much stronger association is noticed amongst those who drink and smoke heavily (OHE 1981).

Circulatory system

Alcohol raises the blood pressure, and some conditions such as alcoholic cardiomyopathy (fatty infiltration of heart muscles) are caused by excessive consumption of alcohol. In the same report of 1981, the OHE reported on a study which found statistically significant associations between alcoholism and many forms of circulatory disease.

Digestive disorders

Alcohol ingestion tends to damage the linings of all the organs in the upper part of the digestive tract, leading to inflammation and often ulceration. Raised death rates amongst alcoholics occur in relation to ulcers of the stomach, duodenum and oesophagus, as well as diseases of the lower intestine. Indeed in 1979 the Royal College of Psychiatrists estimated that some 20% of alcoholics developed peptic ulcers.

Fetal alcohol syndrome

The past twenty years have seen a major increase in concern about the possible harm associated with alcohol consumption during pregnancy. In 1981, the evidence to support the links between such harm and alcohol were judged to be sufficiently persuasive for the United States Surgeon General to issue a warning on the subject. There seems little disagreement with the view that heavy drinking is a definite hazard during pregnancy, and should be avoided before and during pregnancy. However, opinion is divided on the effects of lower drinking levels. Nurses must be cautious about possibly exaggerating the damage that alcohol can cause. The following advice is given to pregnant women in the Health Education Authority's pregnancy book (1988).

> 'Remember that from conception onwards, the less you drink the better your chances of a successful pregnancy and a healthy baby. It is true that if you limit yourself to just an occasional drink, the risk to your baby will be very small. But if you cut out alcohol completely, you cut out this risk completely.'

Liver problems

Donnan and Hickey (1977) indicate the significant relationship between alcohol consumption and liver cirrhosis.

Mental health problems

Alcohol may cause brain atrophy, dementia and Korsakoff's psychosis. Problem drinkers and alcoholics are frequently malnourished and have vitamin deficiencies. Thiamine deficiency may result in the development of amnesia such as Korsakoff's psychosis. Individuals with this problem exhibit serious memory problems. It often occurs following an episode of Wernicke's encephalopathy, symptoms of which include confusion, ataxia and abnormal eye movements. Wernicke's encephalopathy may be treated successfully with large doses of thiamine; but if it progresses to Korsakoff's psychosis, the prognosis for the reversal of memory loss is very poor.

Ritson (1977) states that reports from a number of countries give a range of 6% to 20% for alcoholics who die by suicide.

REFERENCES

Barrison I. G., Viola L., Mumford J., Murray R. M., Gordon M., Murray-Lyon I. M. (1982). Detecting excessive drinking among admissions to a general hospital. *Health Trends*, **14**, 80–3.

Barrison M. D., Levine J., Manheimer M. A. (1974). Cross-national study of the extent of anti-anxiety sedative drug use. *New England Journal of Medicine*, **290**, 769–74.

Davies P., Walsh D. (1983). *Alcohol Problems and Alcohol Control in Europe.* Beckenham: Croom Helm.

Dight S. E. (1976). Scottish Drinking Habits: A Survey of Scottish Drinking Habits and Attitudes Towards Alcohol. Office of Population Census and Surveys. London: HMSO.

DHSS (1977). Advisory Committee on Alcoholism.

Donnan S., Haskey J. (1977). Alcoholism and liver cirrhosis. *Population Trends*, **7**, 18–24.

Edwards G. (1982). *The Treatment of Drinking Problems.* London: Grant McIntyre.

Edwards G. *et al.* (1972). Drinking in a London suburb. *Quarterly Journal of Studies on Alcohol*, supp 6, 69–128.

Galbraith S., Murray W., Patel A., Knill-Jones R. (1976). Relationship between alcohol and head injury and its effects on the conscious level. *British Journal of Surgery*, **66**, 128.

Harvard J. (1977). Alcohol and road accidents. In *Alcoholism: New Knowledge and New Responses.* (Edwards G., Grant M., eds). Beckenham: Croom Helm.

Health Education Authority (1988). *Pregnancy Book.* London: Health Education Authority.

Heather N., Robertson I. (1986). *Problem Drinking.* Harmondsworth: Penguin.

Huss M. (1849). *Icoholismus Chronicus*, Eller Chronisk Atsoholssjukdom.

Jeffs B. W., Saunders W. M. (1983). Minimizing alcohol related offences by enforcement of existing licensing legislation. *British Journal of Addiction*, **78**, 67–77.

Jellinek E. M. (1960). *The Disease Concept of Alcoholism.* New Brunswick: Hillhouse Press.

Keller M. (1960). *Quarterly Journal of Studies on Alcohol*, **2**, 125.

London Weekend Television (1985). *Think Before you Drink.* London Community Unit.

Murray R. (1977). Head injuries and alcohol. In *Alcoholism; New Knowledge and New Responses.* (Edwards G., Grant M., eds). Beckenham: Croom Helm.

Nursing Times (1984). The day the strangers came. 27 June 51–4.

Office of Health Economics (1981). *Alcohol – Reducing the Harm.* Luton: White Crescent.

Office of Population Census and Surveys (1978). *Dicennial Supplement England and Wales on Occupational Mortality.* London: HMSO.

Plant M. A. (1982). *Drinking and Problem Drinking.* London: Junction Books.

Platt S. (1983). *Parasuicide*. Paper presented at the First Scottish School on Drug Problems, Heriot Watt University.

Plaut T. F. (1968). *Alcohol Problems – A Report to the Nation by the Cooperative Commission on the Study of Alcoholism*. Oxford: OUP.

Ritson B. (1977). Alcohol and suicide. In *Alcoholism: New Knowledge and New Responses*. (Edwards G., Grant M., eds). Beckenham: Croom Helm.

Royal College of Psychiatrists (1979). *Alcohol and Alcoholism – Report of the Special Committee of the Royal College of Psychiatrists*. London: Tavistock Publications.

Royal Society for the Prevention of Accidents. (1983). *Annual Report*. London: ROSPA.

Rutherford D. (1988). *A Lot of Bottle*. Cambridge: Tabro Litho.

Spring J. A., Buss D. (1977). Three centuries of alcohol in the British diet. *Nature*, 270, 567–72.

Strathclyde Regional Council. (1981). *Firemaster's Report*. Glasgow: Strathclyde Regional Council.

Taylor D. (1981). *Alcohol – Reducing the Harm*. London: Office of Health Economics.

The Co-operative (1952). Commission on Study of Alcoholism. New York: Oxford Press.

Tyler A. (1984). *Street Drugs*. London: New English Library.

Watson, J. (1979). Glue sniffing. *British Medicine*, 7 November, 31–3.

Wilson P. (1980). *Survey on Drinking in England and Wales*. Office of Population Census and Surveys. London: HMSO.

Chapter 4

General principles of nursing intervention

Having set the scene as to the extent of drug and alcohol problems and reviewed their effects, we consider in this chapter the role of nurses in intervening with people with such problems. Nurses in every setting have an important part to play in dealing with the drug user or problem drinker. This extends from the specialist nurses who are employed in alcohol treatment units or community drug teams, to the non-specialists such as health visitors, nurses in general hospitals and occupational health nurses. It is time for a partnership to be developed between the specialist and non-specialist. We believe that some of the basic techniques of intervention used with people with drug and alcohol problems are not unique to the specialist and can be developed by the non-specialist, provided they have sufficient back-up and support.

Nurses are one of the health care groups who have regular contact with a large amount of people. A proportion of these people may have a drug or alcohol problem. In some situations this may be very obvious, e.g. a young man presenting in the accident and emergency department in an intoxicated state suffering from wound infections at the site of injecting drug use, or a middleaged barman admitted with serious liver problems because of his heavy drinking. At other times, the presentation may not be so obvious. It may take some time for the nurse in the community (whether health visitor or community psychiatric nurse) to realise that a 25-year-old woman is using extra amounts of prescribed minor tranquillisers to cope with life problems, or for the occupational health nurse to identify the trend of an increase in workplace accidents in the afternoon, as a result of lunchtime consumption of alcohol.

We must move away from punitive views of these problems as 'self-inflicted'. In a society where many of our lifestyles can have an adverse effect upon health, it is shortsighted and unrealistic to consider that as people develop serious drug and alcohol problems, they should be left to experience the major physical, psychological and social consequences unaided. Given the incidence of alcohol problems in particular, it is strange that nurses have difficulties in empathising with such patients. Indeed it is very likely that every nurse is aware of relatives, friends or colleagues who have had an alcohol problem. It may be that by acknowledging such problems in our midst, we recognise our own vulnerability, and this appears to be something that the nursing profession finds hard to accept. It is important that we increase our awareness of the patients with these major health problems, and develop the knowledge and skills to enable us to do more than turn a blind eye or adopt a punitive attitude to these patients.

THE SPECIALIST NURSE

Our definition of the specialist nurse is the person who has chosen to work with clients with drug and alcohol problems in a fulltime capacity. This includes nurses in drug dependency units (DDUs) and increasingly within community drug teams. The role of nurses in DDUs has altered since the late 1960s – when the expectations were that they would provide first aid, general nursing care and advice in an outpatient setting to drug users with associated medical problems – to a more holistic approach to people with drug problems. The work of nurses in DDUs has been partly determined by the movement away from the medical model. Nurses are now more likely to provide the kind of assistance that may be in common with their colleagues in the multidisciplinary team, and they also have the advantage of being able to relate changes in treatment to problems that the client is experiencing with physical or psychological withdrawals from the drug. It is clear that there is the potential for blurring of roles in these units, and as working with problem drug users becomes increasingly popular with other professions, nurses need to be sure about their skills and resist attempts to return them to being the first-aider.

Community drug teams are still in an evolutionary stage in the UK, and many have developed as a result of government funding being made available for such services. It appears that these teams are developing somewhat similarly to the model of community alcohol teams, insofar as they usually consist of a fulltime community psychiatric nurse, secretarial support and part-time medical and psychology support. Nurses in these teams play a major role in determining the kind of service provided, since they are often the only fulltime clinical resource. Most community drug teams offer the facility of advice and information (Hunt 1985) as well as support and counselling of individuals and their families (Kumawu 1986). Strang and Creed (1985) report the development of a satellite clinic dealing with people with drug-related problems in Manchester. They outline the role of the community psychiatric nurse in providing community-based supervision and follow-up for patients who are being withdrawn from drugs and still attending clinics, and for those who have stopped clinic attendance. It is noteworthy that the Social Services Committee (1985) report on the misuse of drugs stated 'we consider that it is essential for general practitioners to have the support of an experienced community psychiatric nurse and good liaison with social services if they are to provide an adequate service for drug misusers'. Such recognition and expectations have implications for the level of training, support and clinical career structure that is provided for nurses, and in this speciality it is greatly lacking. It has become commonplace for nurses to join DDUs or community drug teams, work in them for a few years thereby gaining knowledge and developing skills, and then leave to move on to a management role or into the non-statutory sector where advanced skills are often recognised by decent remuneration. This 'brain drain' is very worrying, since it means that just as the level of knowledge and skills is reaching an efficient and effective level, it becomes greatly depleted. The clinical grading structure for nurses, midwives and health visitors may provide opportunities for the matter to be addressed.

Nurses have been a major component of the workforce in alcohol treatment units (ATUs) since they were established and developed in the late 1950s and early 1960s. Despite a much longer time in a specialist role, nurses in the ATUs have continued to experience the same problems as their colleagues in the drug field, especially in relation to training and limited career structure. Our own work has highlighted this, as is evident when Faugier (1981) examined the experience of nurses in a specialised unit for the treatment of alcoholic patients. In her closing discussion she stated 'neither the state enrolled nurse or the registered mental nurse had received any opportunity of in-service training in group techniques'. Despite this, group techniques were the prime mode of therapy within the unit, and a more recent study (Ettore 1984) suggests that group psychotherapy continues to be the most common form of treatment in ATUs. Kennedy (1986) shows that a substantial minority of nurses in charge of ATUs and community alcohol teams plan to move out of this speciality because of the lack of training opportunities and a clinical career structure.

Community alcohol teams developed during the early 1970s, as government policy in England and Wales changed from the goal of highly specialised psychiatric services (i.e. ATUs) to the goal of an integrated community service. These teams usually consist of either a fulltime community psychiatric nurse or social worker supported by a secretary and part-time doctor and/or psychologist. As in the community drug teams, the nurse is expected to undertake an enormous variety of tasks, which may include specialist counselling of clients, advice and information to the general public, and consultation and liaison with other professionals. It is obvious that nurses in this speciality are expected to develop skills and knowledge that are not usually addressed in any depth in their generic training. There is sufficient evidence that these nurses often feel inadequately prepared for this kind of work, and whilst the development of English National Board Course 612 (Drug and Alcohol Dependency Nursing) is welcomed, the issues of adequate support and supervision and clinical career development need to be addressed by such professional organisations as the Association of Nurses in Substance Abuse.

Given the extent of the drug and alcohol problem, it is impossible for the specialist nurse to deal with all the people experiencing difficulties associated with their misuse of drugs or alcohol. In some health authorities there is only one nurse who is seen as the response to drug and alcohol problems. Even in places where such services are well developed, it would still be impossible to deal with all the problems. The specialist nurse has an important role to play in developing a consultative model of work, which provides support and supervision for the non-specialist.

THE NON-SPECIALIST NURSE

Many nurses reading this book may ask, 'Why me, what have I got to offer?' We believe there is considerable evidence to suggest the non-specialist can do much for the person with a drug or alcohol problem. The specific details of the response from these nurses in a variety of settings – the community, the hospital and the workplace – are outlined in Chapter 5. Irrespective of the setting, or the scale of knowledge or skills, there are general principles of nursing intervention for people with drug and alcohol problems; these include:

1 Detection of clients with such problems and responding to them.
2 Helping the clients to acknowledge that they have a problem.
3 Providing the clients with the opportunity to look at the options that are available for them in treatment.
4 Providing nursing care for clients experiencing withdrawal symptoms.
5 Handling relapse.

1 Detection and response

Detecting that somebody has a drug or alcohol problem is not easy. Nurses need to increase their index of suspicion and become more astute at seeing the presenting features or warning signs that somebody may have a drug or alcohol problem. Detection can only take place if a nurse is interested and willing to watch out for these warning signs. This is likely to happen when the nurse feels competent to deal with the difficulties that may arise following an approach to a patient who has a problem. In a hospital setting, there are certain drug and alcohol-related illnesses that in themselves provide clues about a patient's lifestyle. Similarly, associated physical and social difficulties can help to build up a picture of somebody in distress (Table 4.1).

Table 4.1 *Indicators of a possible drug or alcohol problem in an inpatient*

Reasons for admission
  1   Drug or alcohol related illness
  2   Accident proneness – caused by intoxication, leads to frequent visits to accident and emergency department
  3   Blackouts – caused by intoxication and indicated by memory difficulties
  4   Suicide attempt/overdose
  5   Amongst problem drinkers raised liver function tests and mean corpuscular volume for no other reason

Physical problems
  6   Withdrawal symptoms present
  7   Marks on the body unaccountable for, e.g. bruises, cigarette burns
  8   Weight loss due to neglect of diet and money spent on drugs or alcohol rather than food

Social factors
  9   Employment – is the patient in a high-risk occupational group associated with drug or alcohol problems?
 10   Unemployment – what played a part in this? How is the patient dealing with the associated stress?
 11   Hobbies and leisure time – dominated by drug/alcohol related activities
 12   Social disharmony in relationships or family
 13   Convictions for drug or alcohol related offences

In a community setting it can be more difficult to detect the person with a drug or alcohol problem. Patients may try to avoid the visit of a community nurse if they are intoxicated.

The degree of contact and visits by the problem drug user or drinker and their family is often increased because of the large number of medical, psychological and social difficulties experienced (Table 4.2).

Amongst solvent abusers there are certain signs to be aware of. These include the breath smelling of the solvent or chemical; a drunken appearance without the smell of alcohol; a glazed look in the eyes; giggling for no apparent reason; a drowsy and vacant expression; glue stains on clothes; chest pains; cough or permanent cold.

It is important to realise that the indicators outlined in Table 4.2

Table 4.2 *Indicators of a possible drug or alcohol problem in a community setting*

Medical problems
  1 Drug or alcohol related illness
  2 Weight loss due to neglect of diet and money spent on drugs or alcohol rather than food
  3 Vitamin deficiency due to poor diet
  4 Blackouts, bruises and cigarette burns—without satisfactory or consistent account

Psychological difficulties
  5 Irritability and unexplained mood changes
  6 Depression of mood and suicide attempts
  7 Altered sleep pattern

Social problems
  8 Work difficulties
  9 Financial hardship despite apparently adequate income
  10 Convictions for drug or alcohol related offences
  11 Relationship and family problems

should lead to further questioning of the client about the use of a particular substance. A positive response to some of the indicators does not necessarily mean that the person is dependent upon a substance, but might indicate that it is creating problems in their life. In some situations it is necessary to take the risk of offending, in order to find the person with the problem.

In considering how we respond to patients it is useful to think about the service we provide for them. We are, for example, more likely to engage young people in looking at their use of solvents if we work collaboratively with their youth worker, rather than expecting them to attend a DDU. Similarly, as many ATUs are based in large psychiatric hospitals (often many miles from the patient's home and family), it may be that a poor attendance rate has less to do with the patients' motivation and more to do with the patients' feeling that not only do they have an alcohol problem, but also that they are crazy.

DDUs are often based within the precincts of a general hospital, and it is possible that this will reinforce the view of the patient as being passive in the treatment process. Another problem that some DDUs have fallen into is that of treating only people who have problems with a specific drug, i.e. opiates. This implies that if patients have difficulties with, say, cocaine or tranquillisers, there is little that will be offered to them. Such services must realise that the provision of a drug-specific or drug-orientated service often drives an ever-greater wedge between potential clients and the resolution of their difficulties.

Nurses are often only one part of a multidisciplinary team in such services, but at the same time, relatively minor modifications and changes can be made which have few, if any, resource implications. An example is the waiting list. What is the optimal waiting period, or indeed is there one? The Alcohol Problem Advisory Service in Bloomsbury Health Authority (London), showed that a reduction in the waiting period between contact and first appointment played a part in increasing the proportion of attenders at the service. Olkin and Lenle (1984) found that patients scheduled to be seen less than 48 hours after their initial telephone contact were significantly more likely to keep the appointment than those who had to wait longer.

These findings should hardly come as a surprise. Usually it is a crisis or deterioration that facilitates behavioural change: this is true as much for the drug user with supply difficulties, as it is for the heavy smoker who becomes concerned when blood appears in their sputum. We would not say to the smoker, 'Well, this has been a problem for you for the past twenty years, so why should we rush to help you now?' Yet it rolls very smoothly off the tongue when addressed to the drug user or problem drinker. The smoker is usually seen within a week, but the drug user has to wait at least six or seven weeks. In reviewing the kind of response that is provided, whether in a general hospital or a specialist unit, a point of reference is the standard of care that would be acceptable to us, were we in that position. This refers not only to the waiting time but also to where you are seen, by whom (is any choice given to clients about the gender of an interviewer?) and for how long. These practicalities are further reinforced by the model produced by Prochaska and de Clemente (1985) as outlined in Fig.4.1.

Taking a drug/drinking history

Having identified some positive indicators that lead you to suspect that a patient has a drug or alcohol problem, and having obtained some indication that this is true, it is important to take a more detailed history. Such history taking should be completed in a setting where you are unlikely to be interrupted and where patients can be sure that what they say is confidential. The interview should take place in an office away from the ward, rather than in a busy dayroom. The history taker must be in the right frame of mind. There is little point in taking a history if you are feeling angry about the last patient who had been admitted for detoxification. These feelings should be dealt with before making an approach to a new patient.

1 How much of the drug/alcohol is the patient using – including the type, the amount and the frequency?
2 How long has this been happening?
3 Where does the patient use the drug/alcohol?

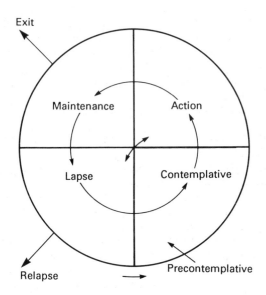

Pre-contemplation: This is the stage when a person is quite happy using drugs and has not begun to contemplate the possibilities of altering their behaviour.

Contemplation: At this stage the person has begun to contemplate the possibilities of altering their drug-using behaviour and may decide to take some action to stop using drugs or they may decide to carry on using.

Action: In the action phase people will usually decide on some course of action which will physically get them off drugs.

Maintenance: It is at this stage that people will usually experience most difficulties as they try to maintain their recent change of behaviour and new-found drug-free state.

Lapse: Because the maintenance stage requires such a lot of work people often have a small setback, i.e. they may use drugs again. However, this need not develop into a full-blown relapse.

Relapse: Should a full-blown relapse develop the person often goes back to a pre-contemplative stage for a while until the next attempt.

Exit: People exit when they have achieved a permanent change in behaviour.

Figure 4.1   *'Motivation to change' model (Prochaska and de Clemente 1984)*

4 With whom does the patient use the drug/alcohol?
5 Does the patient have any feelings before using the drug or alcohol? For example, do they feel angry, depressed or tense, and if so, what effect does the substance have on this feeling?
6 Has the patient ever tried to stop?
7 Has the patient ever previously been worried about the drug or alcohol use?
8 What does the patient see as the positive aspect of the substance abuse?
9 What has been the reaction of family, friends, employers and significant others?
10 What have been the physical, psychological and social consequences of substance use?
11 Is the patient able to identify any significant life events or changes that are connected with commencement or changes in their drug or drinking pattern?
12 Has the patient had any previous contact with helping agencies? If so, when was this and what was the result of such help?

Such questions need to be asked in a manner that is sensitive to the patient's mood, and should not be rushed. If a patient is feeling particularly distressed about one aspect of the history, it is best to leave it and return to it at a later stage when they may feel less distressed. Asking the patient to think in considerable depth about the times in their life when drug or alcohol use was not a problem may help them to focus upon the changes they have to make to achieve this again. This can then lead to a discussion about how some aspects of this time of their life can be recreated. Asking a client to go away and make a very specific and detailed list of these changes is often of value.

A detailed drug or drinking history should be supported by asking the client to complete a diary (Fig.4.2).

The way that questions and statements are used by the interviewer will influence the patient's reaction. For example, 'Every time I call around you smell of alcohol' will elicit a very different response from 'I wonder if there is some difficulty or problem you would like to discuss with me?'

2 Acknowledgement of the problem

We sometimes wonder why clients deny having a problem with a particular substance. In some situations it may be obvious; if you are involved in an illegal activity and admit to it, the potential consequences are predictable. A client who misuses prescribed drugs may not say anything about it, since the likely response of the practitioner is to terminate the supply. A nurse with an alcohol problem may not say

Name ....

DRINKING DIARY (Can be easily adapted for monitoring drug use)

Day/date	Place	Time/who with	No. of units drunk and quantity and type	Describe how you felt before, during and after drinking	Money spent
Sunday					
Monday					
Tuesday					
Wednesday					
Thursday					
Friday					
Saturday					
			Total (units)		Total

Figure 4.2   *Drinking diary (Alcohol Problem Advisory Service)*

anything because of the fear that her career prospects will be damaged. Perhaps it is not so surprising that denial is used by many clients.

Denial is considered to be a defence mechanism, and can best be defined as a mode of irrational or emotionally determined thinking or action which is used as an escape from reality. Normally such defences are unconscious and have the effect of protecting us from overwhelming anxiety. We all use these mechanisms on a day-to-day basis in order to function, and denial is probably one of the most common.

Three reasons why problem drinkers deny their problems are suggested by work at the Hazelden Foundation in the United States. The first is related to our cultural history; as with mental illness, the rationale used over the centuries to explain grossly inappropriate behaviour involved possession by demons (e.g. the 'demon drink') or similar forces of evil. Weinberg describes how this caused a major stigma associated with alcohol problems. This stigma was reinforced by one of the dominant institutions, organised religion, which was powerfully opposed to alcohol, especially in the late nineteenth and early twentieth centuries. This view is concluded thus:

'Alcoholics have historically been regarded as being evil, morally and/or mentally inferior and thus subject to social punishments – disapproval, rejection, ostracism. Who wants to be placed in the category 'alcoholic'?'

The second reason for denial is the social environment. Because drinking is seen generally as a harmless activity, the normal consequences of associated undesirable behaviour are often nothing or merely a minor admonishment the next day by one's partner. Faced with hostility from the drinker and lack of support from relevant others, the partner ignores the behaviour and thereby the drinker gets little sense of reality.

The final reason outlined was intrapsychic consistency. Drinkers are faced with two polarised messages, (a) that alcohol is an important and positive aspect of their life and (b) that its continued use has negative consequences for them.

This work provides some useful material for realising why the process of denial can be such a major influence in behavioural change. There is a grave possibility that acceptance of the denial process by the helper can have a paralysing effect. As Miller (1983) says:

'Within the alcoholism treatment community, "denial" is almost universally described as a pernicious personality characteristic of alcoholics. It is seen as the biggest obstacle to successful treatment and the major reason for treatment failures.'

The other effect of such an acceptance is that the time given over to assisting the client in acknowledging their problem is spent in a mutual battle of wits:

'No, I'm not an alcoholic'

'But yes you are, look at . . .'

As the nurse argues more and more that there is a serious problem, the client gives an opposite view until opinions are totally polarised.

Clients are more likely to give thought to the effects of substance use if feedback about their behaviour or health is given in a clear and understandable way. Patients whose liver disorders are drug or alcohol related will find it easier to accept this when they are helped to understand why the drug or alcohol affects their liver. Many patients say, 'I was told ten years ago I would die if I didn't stop drinking'. This kind of general statement has little impact, but a detailed explanation of their liver function test results is more relevant, especially as the tests can be used as a means of monitoring change and encouraging the client to maintain that change.

Society often endeavours to find distant stereotypes for drug and alcohol problems. The 19-year-old 'junkie' injecting drugs in Piccadilly Circus is much easier to accept than the highly successful businessman using stimulants. The vagrant alcoholics serve a similar function. It is useful to be aware of this labelling when assisting clients in looking at their problems. Energies need to be focused upon explaining that these images are inaccurate and atypical. This is particularly so in providing assistance for people with short-term histories.

3 Looking at the available options for treatment

In Chapter 8 we provide detailed information about the general models of services that should be provided, and a brief list of specific agencies and services that are available is given in the appendix. Before counselling clients in any great depth or detail about the choices that face them, advice from and information about local services is recommended. The amount of progress that you can make in ensuring that clients look at the decisions ahead of them will be primarily determined by their perspective of the problem. Nurses in all settings have a responsibility (especially if they have worked with a client through the process of detection and acknowledgement) to inform clients about the decisions they need to make about their substance use. However, saying 'you must stop' without any more detailed assistance can be counterproductive. Focusing exclusively on the substance ignores the other changes in lifestyle that a client may have to make. This is particularly true for clients who socialise or work in environments where the substance of misuse is an integral part of that activity. Therefore, before discussing options with a client, a clear

Name:	Date:

(a) What happens if I continue to take heroin:

     positive: have friends
                         keep happy
                         keep my girlfriend
                         etc.

     negative: stay broke
                         maybe be ill
                         get in trouble with police
                         etc.

(b) What happens if I stop heroin:

     positive: feel better physically
                         have some money
                         etc.

     negative: get withdrawals
                         lose my friends and accommodation
                         etc.

Figure 4.3   *Balance sheet of choices*

knowledge of the environment and pressures that influence the use of the drug or alcohol is essential.

A particular way of encouraging a client to focus upon their choices, and probable consequences is to develop a balance sheet. This provides a personal means of identifying what the future may hold. The example outlined in Fig.4.3 provides some evidence to the client of what will probably happen depending upon what choice he makes. In this case, physical health or symptoms and the status of friends are important factors.

The balance sheet should be completed by the clients in their own time, since it is important that they judge and determine what is important. The nurse can then discuss the balance sheet, and assist the client in exploring at greater length the significance of factors identified. It may also be possible to outline for the clients how they can deal with the consequences. For example, in the case of withdrawal symptoms, details can be made available of how the symptoms can be treated or alleviated.

It is useful to recall the advice from *Treatment and Rehabilitation* (DHSS 1982):

'The aim should be (a) to enable problem drug takers to utilize personal resources and so modify attitudes, behaviour and skills to achieve a more stable and fulfilling way of life with minimal or no drug related problems; (b) to provide the social supports and agencies required to facilitate the development of the individual so as to establish or re-establish problem drug takers in the community in roles which they find more stable and fulfilling than those related to their previous drug use.'

4 Nursing care during withdrawal from drugs or alcohol

Withdrawal symptoms associated with many drugs are characterised by rebound effects in some physiological systems that were modified by the drugs – *rebound hyperexcitability*. Traditionally, the treatment of withdrawal symptoms (detoxification) has been seen as a vital component of any change made by the client. This is to some extent true. However, not every client experiences withdrawal symptoms upon cessation of a drug, and if the process of detoxification is focused upon to the exclusion of all else, clients will get the impression that once it has been completed, so too has treatment.

Any intervention associated with the management of withdrawal needs to be carefully monitored. This should take place in collaboration with a medical practitioner, either the client's general practitioner or a hospital physician. In taking a drug or drinking history, the nurse

Day		1	2	3	4	5	6	7	8	9	10
1 Appetite	a.m.										
	p.m.										
2 Sleep pattern	a.m.										
	p.m.										
3 Tremor	a.m.										
	p.m.										
4 Sweating	a.m.										
	p.m.										
5 Gastric disturbance	a.m.										
	p.m.										
6 Anxiety	a.m.										
	p.m.										
7 Concentration	a.m.										
	p.m.										
8 Craving	a.m.										
	p.m.										

1 : No problem
5 : Mild problem
10 : Serious problem

Figure 4.4 *Monitoring diary of withdrawals*

should identify with the client the experiences (physical and psychological) associated with abstinence. In an outpatient or community setting, this can be further assisted by asking a client to attend an appointment having been abstinent for several hours. Amongst problem drinkers, the level of withdrawal symptoms can be correlated with a breath alcohol content by using a breathalyser. This can be further explored by asking clients to keep a diary to monitor the symptoms they experience (Fig.4.4).

Hospital detoxification

If the assessment takes place in hospital, the diary can be used to trigger the patient's memory and may elicit valuable information.

The place where detoxification occurs is determined by the level of dependence upon the substance. If a client has experienced such symptoms as withdrawal fits or seizures, paranoid feelings or hallucinations, then admission to hospital where there is sufficient nursing care and medical help is indicated. It should be made clear to the client that abstinence from the substance whilst in hospital is expected. It is useful to clarify this arrangement by a contract (Fig.4.5).

The following conditions form a framework with which it is possible for us to assist you to detoxify. If at any stage you cannot accept these conditions, you are of course free to leave and indeed if you break this contract you will be asked by the staff to leave.

1 No consumption of drugs/alcohol during stay.
2 No medication to be brought into hospital (all medication will be prescribed by hospital staff).
3 Inform all visitors that they are not to bring drugs/alcohol into the hospital.
4 While detoxifying patients are expected to stay on the ward.
   I have read these conditions.

   Signed.....................
   Date.....................

Figure 4.5 *Detoxification contract*

A contract is useless unless there is unanimity amongst the medical and nursing team about its implementation. The aim is to provide a method by which all involved have as clear a structure as possible to work in. Surprisingly, the majority of clients respond very positively to the presence of a contract. Often they have been the recipient of extremely subtle or vague messages about their substance use, whereas the contract provides a clear and tangible indication of the consequences of certain behaviour. A copy should be given to the client and a copy kept in the case notes.

Community detoxification
Detoxification from drugs or alcohol can also take place in a community setting. This is particularly suitable for clients who have mild withdrawal symptoms. Amongst drug users, withdrawal may be spread over several weeks, whereas with problem drinkers the programme is much shorter. In addition to assessing the level of physical dependence, the nurse should be certain before embarking on a community detoxification that the client has adequate support at home, in the form of a relative or friend who is prepared to provide assistance during this time. Also, if the prescribing is not being completed by the client's general practitioner, he or she should be kept closely informed about progress and level of prescribing, so that if complications arise (especially at night or weekends) the most suitable treatment can be initiated. Any drugs prescribed during this stage need to be carefully monitored, since several of those used (especially in alcohol detoxification) have addictive properties. The client should be given a day's supply at a time, and when more than a day's supply has to be given out (e.g. at bank holidays or weekends) then the assistance of the relative or friend in such monitoring should be requested. It is recommended that a community detoxification should commence several days before the end of the working week, and avoid long bank-holiday weekends when access to services is difficult.

Benzodiazepine detoxification
The management of withdrawal from dependence on benzodiazepines generally occurs in an outpatient setting. The exceptions to this are patients on high doses, and those with a history of fits or psychotic episodes during previous attempts at withdrawal. In some situations where a client has been prescribed a short-acting benzodiazepine, it is replaced by a long-acting one as there is then a more gradual reduction in levels of the drug.

Diaries can also be used by patients to monitor symptoms, and thus provide suggestions about the actual precipitants to stress and tranquilliser use.

Drugs used in detoxification
The prescribing of drugs to treat withdrawal symptoms does sometimes give the client a mixed message. At one moment they are told that they must stop using a particular drug, and the next minute they are handed a prescription for a different drug. It should be made clear that the

prescribing is short-term and is specific to the management of withdrawal symptoms.

A great variety of drugs is used in the treatment of withdrawal symptoms from drugs and alcohol. We have provided information on those that are most commonly used.

Chlormethiazole (Heminevrin) is a hypnotic drug used in the treatment of acute alcohol withdrawal symptoms. It has considerable addictive properties and should only be prescribed under strict supervision. It is recommended that treatment is not carried on for more than nine days. It is available in capsule, syrup and injecting form. The risks associated with the long-term use of chlormethiazole are considerable, as outlined by Caviston *et al.* (1988). These risks include its action being potentiated by other sedatives such as alcohol; long-term dependence is almost inevitable, and withdrawal is extremely difficult and dangerous.

Chlordiazepoxide (Librium) is a benzodiazepine that has become popular in the treatment of acute alcohol withdrawal symptoms. There is relatively little danger of respiratory depression with benzodiazepines. It is available in tablet, capsule and injecting form.

Methadone (Physeptone) has proved successful for the detoxification of clients experiencing dependence on opiates.

Diazepam (Valium) has strong anticonvulsant effects and can be of assistance prophylactically (preferably) or acutely in the management of withdrawal fits.

Advice to client
The following advice, from a leaflet prepared by the Alcohol Problem Advisory Service of Bloomsbury Health Authority for clients completing a community detoxification, provides a useful checklist of areas to be discussed.

Time off: if you are working, try to take at least two weeks off – your GP may be willing to help with this.

Safety: you may feel shaky and/or drowsy. Avoid anything which may cause an accident, e.g. pouring boiling water, bathing, etc. *Do not drive or operate machinery.*

Hygiene: regular washing, especially if excessive sweating occurs.

Environment: find somewhere quiet, calm and comfortable. You may feel irritable and oversensitive to light and noise.

Psychological: concentration may be difficult at first but try to have plenty to keep you occupied – reading, hobbies, etc. Try not to sleep during the day, although you should rest as much as possible.

Diet: you may not feel like eating much during the first few days, so drink plenty as you may become dehydrated. Water is an excellent thirst quencher. Squash may be added although orange juice can irritate nausea. Milk is good for digestive problems. Meals should be small, regular, and include plenty of protein and vitamins, e.g. fruit, vegetables, fish, eggs, cheese, liver, etc.

Drugs: take your medication as prescribed. It will be monitored throughout the programme and adjusted as necessary.

Remember: a detoxification programme is only the first step in your recovery. The next stage is *staying stopped*. During the programme we will look at ways which can help and support you to remain abstinent from alcohol, if that is your goal; e.g. group therapy, individual counselling.

5 Handling relapse

Relapse is the return of the client to substance use. The effect of relapse can be extremely traumatic both for the client and nurse. For the client it can mean feeling depressed and dejected as a result of seeing many days, weeks or years of sobriety blown. This emotion is often reinforced and made even greater by the intervention of health care workers. We feel angry that the client has 'failed'.

Historically, having a drug or alcohol problem was viewed as a disease and the 'sick' addicts were seen as having no control over their problem. By implication relapses were seen as part of this spectrum.

More recently, alternative explanations have been developed. Bandura (1969) has explained addiction and relapse within a framework of social learning theory. Addictive behaviours are viewed through the principles of social learning, cognitive psychology and behaviour modification. This model has been further developed by Marlatt (1978), who argues that addictive behaviours temporarily give rise to positive feelings in the individual, but in the longer term produce detrimental effects that may be physical, social or psychological. Marlatt has coined the term 'apparently irrelevant decisions' to describe the process of making a series of decisions that increase the likelihood of the person encountering a situation where the risk of relapse is high. Such decisions might include an ex-heroin user arranging a meeting with somebody who is currently using, or a client who has stopped using tranquillisers keeping a small supply for her mother who has not stopped.

Once in this high-risk situation (Fig.4.6) clients face a major choice. If they have a coping response and are able to initiate it, the feelings experienced will be positive and self-congratulatory – referred to by Bandura as 'self efficacy'. However, clients may experience high-risk situations that are unexpected or that they are unprepared for. As they become conscious of their predicament a reduction in self efficacy is evident, often associated with the expectation that use of the substance will make the negative feelings disappear. This leads to initial use of the

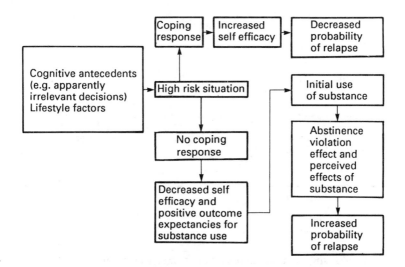

Figure 4.6 *Cognitive behavioural model of relapse*

substance and the abstinence violation effect. At this stage, memories associated with lack of control are recalled, e.g. 'One drink, one drunk'. Thus the decrease in self efficacy is reinforced and the probability of relapse made greater.

In handling relapse it is useful to be able to identify the high-risk situations. Amongst a sample of alcoholics, Cummings *et al.* (1980) identified the following as high-risk relapse situations: negative emotional states (38%), interpersonal conflict (18%), social pressure (18%) and urges/temptations. Amongst heroin addicts the situations were social pressures (36%), negative emotional states (19%), interpersonal conflict (14%) and positive emotional states (10%).

There are many stages at which relapse can be prevented. A good starting point is an acknowledgement on the part of the nurse that the risk of relapse is a reality. To acknowledge this not only privately, but also to the client, can prepare the ground for the client's return should they relapse. The next stage is to get the clients to look at the high-risk situations, asking them to use a diary to help identify stimuli or cues to the relapse, e.g. certain surroundings or friends. When clients feel vulnerable or uneasy, they may associate these different influences. Despite this identification, the client is likely to encounter high-risk situations and will therefore need adequate coping responses. By using modelling and skills training, clients can generate and maintain the skills which result in less frequent and severe relapses. Desensitisation can also be used to expose the client gradually to these situations. If clients use the substance they should be advised to seek help. Cummings

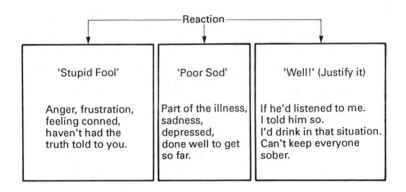

Figure 4.7   *The effect of relapse on the therapist*

et al. (1980) suggest that clients be instructed to wait at least 20 minutes after the initial urge to relapse before acting on any decision to do so. This focuses the client's attention on the process of making a decision.

The effect of relapse on the therapist can be considerable. Stonard (1986) outlines some of the reactions (Fig.4.7). The variety of reactions is not surprising. The amount of personal investment often has been considerable, both in respect of actual hours of work and level of emotional work completed. Nurses as a result may question their own ability, wondering if they could have done more, and if they are effective at what they do. Such feelings highlight the importance of proper supervision for this work. Some of the following measures may help to deal with these effects:

1   Accept that such feelings are natural.
2   Convert the feelings into positive action.
3   Let go – only the client can decide when he or she stops.
4   Don't take it home with you.
5   If you feel you could have done better or were in error, find someone safe and reliable to talk it through with.
6   Learn from it (but don't damage yourself on an inquest).
7   See other clients who are doing well.
8   Tell the client that all is not lost.
9   Remember that a relapse can be just as educational to the client as a period of sobriety can be.

Following a relapse, try to stand back and see what has happened. We sometimes do not realise that the behaviour and reactions of professionals can play a role in relapse, as the following case study illustrates.

Case history

Jenny is a 55-year-old woman who lives alone in an inner-city council flat. She was diagnosed as an alcoholic some twenty years ago. During this time, she has attended several alcohol treatment units and has also been to the local psychiatric units, all to no avail. As her social conditions worsened and her mental state deteriorated, she started being visited regularly by a social worker and community psychiatric nurse. They became increasingly concerned as the frequency of her relapses increased and the periods of abstinence became shorter. As a result, she was falling behind with the payment of bills and was unwell physically.

A visit from a member of the local CAT identified several possible reasons why Jenny relapsed so frequently. One of these was that during times when she was sober, the social worker and community psychiatric nurse did not visit. They did not see any reason to. Visits were targeted at times when she had relapsed.

It was apparent that unconsciously the workers were reinforcing Jenny's drinking behaviour. Her only mechanism of gaining visits and help was by drinking; when sober she was lonely and isolated. It was recommended that the workers should change their response and react at times of abstinence, by visiting Jenny more frequently. After a short while, the pattern began to change and relapses became less frequent.

REFERENCES

Bandura A. (1969). *Principles of Behaviour Modification.* New York: Holt Rinehart & Winston.

Barrison I. G., Viola L., Mumford J., Murray R. M., Gordon M., Murray-Lyon I. M. (1982). Detecting excessive drinking among admissions to a general hospital. *Health Trends,* **14**, 80–3.

Caviston P., McGregor I., Paton A. (1988). Chlormethiazole and alcohol abuse. *Practitioner,* **232**, 217.

Chick J., Lloyd G., Crombie E. (1985). Counselling problem drinkers in medical wards: a controlled study. *British Medical Journal,* **290**, 965–7.

Cummings C., Gordon J. R., Marlatt G. A. (1980). In *The Additives Behaviour; Treatment of Alcoholism, Drug Abuse, Smoking and Obesity,* (Miller W. R. ed) Oxford: Pergamon Press.

DHSS. (1982). *Treatment and Rehabilitation.* Report of the Advisory Council on the Misuse of Drugs. London: HMSO.

Ettore E. M. (1984). A study of alcoholism treatment units: treatment activities and the institutional response. Unpublished paper. London: Addiction Research Unit.

Faugier J. M. (1981). Experience of nursing in a specialised unit for the treatment of alcoholic patients. MA Dissertation. Department of Nursing, Manchester University.

Hunt W. G. (1985). *Community Drug Advice Service.* Unpublished report of Barking, Havering and Brentwood Health Authority. London.

Kennedy J. (1986). The previous training and present training needs of nurses in charge of alcohol treatment units and community alcohol teams. *Journal of Advanced Nursing,* **11**, 283–8.

Kumawu N. (1986). *DASH – A Progress Report*. Unpublished report of Drug Advisory Service, Haringey, London.

Marlatt G. A. (1978). Craving for alcohol, loss of control and relapse: a cognitive behavioural analysis. In *Alcoholism: New Directions In Behavioural Research and Treatment* (Nathan P. E., Marlatt G. A, Loberg T., eds). New York: Plenum Publishing.

Miller W. R. (1983). Motivational interviewing with problem drinkers. *Behavioural Psychotherapy*, **11**, 147–72.

Olkin R., Lenle R. (1984). Increasing attendance in an outpatient alcoholism clinic: a comparison of two intake procedures. *Journal of Studies on Alcohol*, **45** (5), 465–8.

Phillips K. (1986). Neonatal drug addicts. *Nursing Times*, 19 March, 36–8.

Prochaska J. O., de Clemente C. (1985). Common processes of change for smoking, weight control and psychological distress. In *Coping and Substance Abuse* (Schiffman S., Wills T., eds). New York: Academic Press.

Social Services Committee. (1985). *Misuse of Drugs*. London: HMSO.

Strang J. S., Creed F. H. (1985). *Treatment of drug dependence – role of the satellite clinic. Health Trends*, **17**(1), 17–18.

Stonard A. (1986). The effect of relapse on the therapist. Unpublished paper of Rugby House Project. London.

Chapter 5

Longer-term interventions with clients

Some clients presenting with problems of substance abuse often require longer-term intervention by nurses specially trained and experienced in interpersonal techniques. The vehicle of delivery for much of this longer-term treatment is the relationship established between the client and the nurse specialist. Developing such a relationship poses problems with many types of clients, but substance abusers often cause more than their fair share of frustrations and disappointments. In the previous chapter, we discussed the nursing intervention necessary to help clients stop using a particular substance, or to assist them in gaining more control of its use. This, however, only constitutes a tiny step on the road to a 'normal' life. Often the use of drugs has been but a screen to cope with a whole host of problems often stemming from earlier experiences and interpersonal issues. Alternatively, substance abuse may have led clients into behaviour and activities which, once they have stopped taking the drug, give them feelings of shame and guilt.

As a result of drug use, clients may have lost everything which most of us hold dear in life: family, relationships, job, home, security; often all they are left with is the drug and, after the withdrawal period, even that disappears. It should not surprise us that many clients enter a stage of grieving for all the loss that substance abuse can ultimately entail.

Following withdrawal, and the stages of dealing with the physical effects of the substance, clients are left to pick up the pieces, and to deal with the issues, still unresolved, which perhaps contributed to the problems in the first place. Often these issues are less than obvious to clients, and all they have is the question why – 'Why me?' 'Why am I like this?' 'Why did I need to use drugs (or alcohol)?' Their feelings about themselves can reach a very low point and self-esteem will be hard to re-establish.

It is at this stage that the nurse therapist will be involved in what Edwards (1982) refers to as the 'basic work' of treatment. This involves the building of a therapeutic alliance with the client, a relationship built on honesty, trust and warmth. Although it is difficult to summarise all the aspects of this basic work, we attempt here to outline the fundamentals; although the personalities of the nurse and of the client will be important in deciding the quality of what takes place between them, there are certain aspects of the interaction that need to be professionally developed. First of all, both parties must have some commitment to the encounter, and the relationship must positively matter to them. Only then will what the therapist says or does become, as it must, subjectively important to the client. Edwards (1982) claims that work with substance abuse requires the development of a very practised awareness of how relationships are made and used.

One of the ways in which the nurse can lay these essential foundations lies in the use of sensitive and sympathetic communication and conversational skills. It is possible to draw on a highly successful model of conversation used in psychotherapy in order to improve these facets of our intervention.

Although, as Kaufman (1979) points out, pure psychodynamic therapy has rarely been applied to substance abusers because they usually require a much more active limit-setting emphasis, we can improve our interaction by using psychodynamic techniques.

A model used extensively in short-term and long-term therapy, and with universal application in terms of communication, is the conversational model of psychotherapy developed by Hobson (1986), designed to aid the therapy of clients whose problems lie in intimate relationships, in 'knowing' people as distinct from 'knowing about' people or things. Past deprivations, hurts and failures result in:

1   Lack of opportunity to learn a language in which personal feelings can be expressed, understood and shared.
2   Crippling activities (e.g. substance abuse) used to avoid fearful, painful situations reflected in disorders of behaviour.

The process of therapy is termed 'personal problem solving'; this means the discovery, exploration and solution of significant problems which are directly enacted in the 'here and now' of the therapeutic conversation.

A personal conversation, promoted in therapy, involves the differentiation and integration of many forms of language – modes of being with people. The crucial language of 'knowing' is one that expresses and communicates feelings.

The basic building blocks of this model are:

1   An apprehension of, and 'staying with', immediate experience, especially by the use of symbols, for example figurative language and metaphor.
2   Owning experiences (especially in relation to people, i.e. thoughts, wishes, feelings) in a movement from passivity to

activity, characterised by accepting responsibility for acts formerly disclaimed by avoidance activities associated with conflict.

3 Mutual correction of misunderstanding by adjustment of ineffective communication and promotion of dialogue.

4 Learning different ways of achieving personal 'knowing', especially by dealing with misunderstanding.

Any nurse utilising an interpersonal approach should look into the important skills and techniques involved in the use of this model. What follows is only a brief description of some of the techniques Hobson has continued to refine, and the reader is directed towards his own full and vital description of their use (Hobson 1986).

Setting and structure

It is essential that the nurse therapist gives attention to the 'language' of the setting in which the sessions with clients take place. To facilitate therapeutic conversation, identical chairs should be set at an angle, enabling both eye contact and its avoidance, if wished. Not enough attention is given to this factor; encounters with clients often take place in 'any old room', with frequent interruptions giving a feeling of intrusion, or in a different room each time, which does not give clients the time to feel settled in familiar surroundings. Attention to the setting can be a crucial factor in providing a 'safe' environment within which the client can confront painful issues.

'I' and 'we'

Using the terms 'I' and 'we' instead of the more usual 'you' indicates that two people are involved in a mutual exploration of the problems. It also conveys a sense of togetherness, whilst affirming the separateness of the therapist and client.

Statements

Questions can be an implication that the client is being subjected to an interrogation, which can inhibit mutual exploration. By avoiding direct questions, the therapist will be less likely to put the client on the spot about deep interpersonal issues. Direct questioning at this stage of a relationship may simply result in the client closing down further those painful areas that are difficult to deal with. Statements, if appropriately made, are open to correction by the client. They provide a starting point from which diverging themes can develop.

Negotiation

The important part of a conversation is often not so much what is said but rather *how* it is said. The therapist's tone should be 'tentative'. Hobson (1986) states that to be tentative is not to be vague; the therapist is really conveying that he or she does not have the right answer for the patient and is open to correction. Acknowledgement of misunderstandings should occur for a developing relationship to progress.

Here and now

In order to help the client deal with feelings, it is essential that the therapist develops the skill of working in the 'here and now'. All too often, clients will avoid their real feelings by reporting their 'story' in some historical, chronological fashion, which they can talk about as if it happened to someone else because they are not feeling it. The therapist's task is to attempt to get the client to stay with what it 'feels' like and to experience it in the here and now of the conversation.

The use of hypotheses

The therapist puts forward hypotheses based on issues from the patient as well as on his or her own experience and knowledge. Cues from the patient may be verbal or nonverbal (gestures, facial expressions, etc.). The hypotheses floated by the therapist are simply tentative ways of promoting the exploration and organisation of feeling.

Listening and noticing

The most vital part of the therapist's role is to listen and to go on learning how to listen, not only to the client but also to the therapist's own internal response to the client. This includes the ability to 'notice' actively certain particulars of the interaction, at the same time remaining open to other cues and communication.

The therapeutic interview

The beginning of the interview sets the scene for what is to follow.

1. Introduce yourself.
2. Specify the overall purpose of the interview.
3. Indicate the time available for the interview.
4. Comment on the situation and make a guess at how the client is feeling (this shows that you are interested in the patients' feelings and may help them to relax a little).

The following is an example of an interview with a patient referred by his general practitioner to the community drug nurse specialist. The interview is taking place in a private consulting room at the health centre.

Nurse   Hello, Mr Brown; thank you for coming to see me today. You know that your doctor asked me to see you.

Patient   Yes – I am not sure what it's all about. The doctor thinks I am taking too many pills.

Nurse   Well, perhaps it would help if you told me something about how you see things, something about the problems you may want some help with.

Patient   I am not really sure – I don't feel as if I know where to start.

Nurse   OK. Take your time; I know you must feel a bit anxious being asked to come here to talk to me like this. (*Acknowledgement of patient's feelings*)

Patient   I have tried to talk to the doctor at the surgery but she is always so busy – there are other patients waiting; I feel that I am taking up her time.

Nurse   Well, perhaps you will find it easier here. We have the next 45 minutes to talk about the matters which are worrying you, if that is OK. (*A clear indication to the patient of the time available*)

Patient   Yes, that's fine.

Nurse   Perhaps you could start by telling me how the problem started.

Patient   It's hard to describe really – but when I was 45, the firm I worked for closed down and I was made redundant. I thought I would get another job, but application after application got nowhere.

Nurse   That sounds quite painful – being rejected so often like that. (*Focus on the patient's feelings rather than the details of the story*)

Patient   Well, yes – I thought I was coping with it but things got progressively worse at home – worry about bills, etc. I have always been the breadwinner, but now my wife is the one who keeps the family and I am at home all day. It has caused problems between us.

Nurse   I guess that you feel guilty in some way – as if you have let them down. (*Again, the nurse focuses on difficult emotional feelings, and this gives the patient permission to talk about them in a safe, accepting environment*)

Patient   Well, I got depressed really and when I went to the doctor's I couldn't really talk about it. She gave me some

	pills – tranquillisers – and at first they helped, but I started to take more than I should. When my wife went to work and the children had left for school, I would take two or three instead of one – sometimes I would wash them down with a drink – they would help me sleep the day away, to block everything out.

Nurse You were trying to block everything out. I wonder if you could tell me a bit more about how that felt. (*The nurse reflects this back and asks the patient to examine and stay with this feeling for a while*)

Patient I don't feel able to cope most of the time, and my wife and I have stopped even talking about it. She knows I am different and that something is wrong but she doesn't know about the pills and the drinking. She just gets mad when she comes home and the housework isn't done.

Nurse It sounds as if you find it difficult to admit that you are not coping.

Patient Well – I always was the strong one; my work was important and well paid. I was the one who used to take decisions and spend time away from home. Now all I do is sleep all day, taking pills and drinking; I can hardly believe that this has happened to me.

Nurse *I wonder* if the problem is not only that your wife finds it difficult to cope with the changes, but also that you have not really accepted what happened: the loss of job, your new role in the house, etc. (*The tentative nature of this statement makes it* negotiable *with the patient – he is able to accept and pursue the idea or reject it*)

Patient Even when it was happening at work, I didn't really think it would. We all knew that the firm was in trouble but I denied it for months – didn't really face the real situation.

Nurse Sounds as though that might be something that you often do – deny that things are as bad as they are – I suppose the pills and the drink help you to continue this sometimes.

Patient Yes, and it's just getting worse now, I am lying to the family and the doctor.

Nurse And perhaps more importantly to yourself?

Patient Yes – but I don't know what else to do, and when I don't take so many pills I get so anxious I feel as if I am going to go mad.

Nurse That sounds really frightening – as if you feel quite powerless. (*Once again, in a totally non-judgemental way, the nurse acknowledges the patient's feelings – empathising with his predicament*)

Patient I am really; there doesn't seem to be anything I can do.

Nurse	Maybe *we* can look at ways of helping you to work out some ways of coping. Initially, maybe, simply helping you to talk about the problems instead of bottling them up – how does that sound?
Patient	I certainly can't go on like this.
Nurse	Well, I would suggest that we meet twice a week for an hour for the next six weeks and then review your progress. And for this week, I would like you to think about the times when you use the pills and the alcohol more often than others. Maybe we could chat about what's going on inside you at those times.
Patient	OK. I don't think it will be easy, but I am willing to give it a try.

In this short extract from an initial session, we have shown that it is possible, by using a therapeutic model, to build a rapport and focus on patients' feelings by creating an atmosphere in which a discussion of substance abuse problems becomes easier. In this way, the nurse is able to establish a contract with the patient and an agreement to try to work on the problems.

The use of such a model is not outlined here as a call to get involved in interpretive psychodynamic psychotherapy with every substance abuser you come across, but simply as a very effective battery of communication skills for the ongoing long-term work of examining painful underlying issues. Edwards (1982) states:

'It is inappropriate to concentrate on exploration of, say, early relationships and go towards a form of an orthodox psychodynamic approach with relative lack of structure and interpretations, while work problems take second place. But it would also be mistaken to concentrate on why a patient is in perpetual confrontation with superiors at work without exploring his lifelong difficulties with authority.'

The interaction should be concerned with the client's realities and immediate concerns, but the therapist should also remain constantly aware of 'inevitable psychodynamic implications'.

Other interactive models useful in the treatment of substance abusers are counselling models. The term 'counselling' has come to cover a multitude of different interpersonal communicative modes of working with clients, and sceptics might argue that it is now almost as frequently prescribed as Valium! Within a wide spectrum, counselling models vary from a very non-directive approach, as developed by Carl Rogers to a more behavioural approach in which counsellors are involved in goal-setting and reinforcement. However, for our purposes, it is probably sufficient to define counselling as a relationship through which the counsellor seeks to help the client live more effectively and cope more appropriately with various problems. Nelson-Jones (1983) says that the hallmarks of a counselling relationship are (1) empathic understanding, and (2) active listening (Fig.5.1).

Position A	Position B
The counsellor as a person: counselling is above all a good human relationship	The counsellor as a technical expert: above all the application of technical skills

Position C

The counsellor as a caring person with special skills: counselling is a combination of human relating as well as other helping skills

Figure 5.1   *Views of the counsellor and counselling (Nelson-Jones 1983)*

Edwards (1982) reiterates some of the hallmarks needed by the nurse counsellor/therapist in any interaction skill with substance-abusing clients.

1 Warmth and acceptance
This is difficult to achieve if the nurses expected to make a long-term commitment to such clients have not sorted out their own feelings towards them. The clients will arrive for treatment with an expectation of rejection, something they have probably already experienced from other professionals. By using the skills of voice and gesture outlined earlier, the nurse can avoid this disruptive influence and go on to establish a working alliance.

2 Positiveness and direction
Substance-abusing clients often feel like a piece of driftwood in a storm, without any sense of where they are headed, and helpless to do anything to gain control. Even after they achieve abstinence, there usually remains the major issue of how to make sense of the mess that is left in their life. It is necessary to strike a careful balance here between giving some direction, and creating dependence on the therapist and on the therapist's ideas and directions. The clients' calls for help can be so easily responded to by placing them in a dependent 'sick note' situation,

which can prove disastrous to the future of any therapeutic endeavours. Too much direction does nothing to encourage the client's autonomy. Therapists must identify the subtle but essential difference between telling clients what to do, and reinforcing the clients' own ideas about what they can and would like to do.

Conferring warmth and hope

Clients are all too often riddled with hopelessness and guilt, and to have someone believe in them usually marks a turning point in their treatment. The only way to help clients overcome those destructive feelings over a period of time is for their therapist to keep showing that she or he has time for them; that is the only way to convey to them the belief that they can make it through.

Behavioural approaches to substance misuse

Behavioural treatment methods rest firmly on the premise that what needs to be altered is the client's behaviour. On the surface, this appears to contradict the psychodynamic view which contends that the behaviour is merely a symptom, albeit an important and destructive one, especially in substance abuse. However, as Edwards (1982) perceptively states:

'The closer one gets to the care and understanding of the individual patient, the less meaningful does any confrontation between supposedly opposite philosophies become.'

Nurses working in long-term treatment of substance abusers must be generalists, willing to accept that their preferred form of intervention is not always the right one for the client. A psychodynamically orientated nurse will need to be able to recognise where facets of the patients' problems would respond more effectively to a behavioural approach. Similarly, the skilled behaviour therapist should be able to recognise the 'meaning' of substance abuse for the individual as well as being concerned with manifest behaviour.

Social skills training

Many clients, both drug and alcohol abusers, use their drug of choice to deal with an underlying problem of social anxiety. For many years, these clients may have misused a substance as a means of gaining the courage to face anxiety-provoking social occasions. Sometimes all they lack is a little self-esteem and confidence. Other clients may never have properly learned the skills needed to feel at ease in such gatherings. Behavioural approaches can take clients step by step through a process of desensitisation which exposes them to those dreaded occasions, at first through role-playing exercises, and then perhaps by means of controlled *in vivo* situations.

Assertion training

Similarly, many clients are so lacking in a sense of themselves that they are unable, within a peer group or an interpersonal relationship, to assert themselves and make their real wishes known, which renders them easy to manipulate and erodes their already poor sense of self-worth. Assertion skills will be essential after detoxification, when the ability to say 'no' to certain offers becomes vital.

With the use of role play and reinforcement techniques, behaviour therapy can develop skills to increase assertiveness, self-esteem and self-knowledge, all essential facets which strengthen the client's chances of staying drug free.

Relaxation

Drugs and alcohol are often used to achieve relaxation, at enormous cost. Clients who are chronically tense can no longer rely on other, less damaging, ways of relaxing. This leads to a 'vicious circle', in which tension produces drug use, which makes the client later feel bad, guilty and tense; answer: more drugs.

For nurses using relaxation techniques, biofeedback mechanisms can break this destructive cycle and assist the client towards developing healthier ways of relaxing, such as yoga and transcendental meditation.

Cognitive approaches

These approaches to a whole range of psychiatric conditions have shown great value in the past decade and certainly are helpful to some clients with dependency problems. The theory of 'cognitive restructuring', primarily used with depressed people, is based on the assumption that irrational beliefs and distorted ideas influence people's ability to change their behaviour. These techniques have been widely applied in the alcohol field with encouraging results. Problem drinkers who firmly hold the belief that the substance, rather than themselves, controls the progression of their drinking careers, obviously find it difficult to exert any influence or to have any real belief in their ability to stop or cut down.

In practice, the clients are encouraged to identify realistic goals and use group discussion to work out 'cognitive restructuring' in relation to their achievement. A major strength of this approach to dependency is that, unlike many others, it takes on board the challenge of relapse.

Relapse is a common problem for nurses working with this client group, and a model that acknowledges this has distinct advantages. Clients can, during treatment, be faced with situations that will place them in danger of relapsing, and they will be able to practise and 'rehearse' strategies to cope. This approach to bringing relapse out into the open helps them to deal better with it, should it happen. Rollnick (1985): 'Relapse prevention techniques are also able to help clients deal with a return to drinking and prevent the possibility of a lapse developing into a full-blown relapse.'

Cognitive restructuring techniques can assist clients to view a lapse for what it is, instead of a major personal disaster and a betrayal of the trust placed in them by professional workers. Often when a lapse takes place following treatment, the individual is filled with guilt and views the incident as the inevitable start of a return to drinking on the scale it was prior to treatment. It is essential that clients have the opportunity to examine their beliefs about these incidents *before* they happen.

Controlled or normal drinking

Some clients with drinking problems may be helped by the therapeutic team to establish normal drinking patterns. More and more clients are now seen by nurses at an early stage in the development of dependency, and the prospect of years or even decades of sobriety, in a society which often seems obsessed by alcohol, can be unattractive and unrealistic.

Not all clients are suitable for inclusion in such a programme. Those who suffer from underlying mental illness and use alcohol in order to deal with emotional pain are unlikely to be able to develop the necessary control without treatment of the underlying disorder. Clients who are polydrug users are also poor candidates unless the drug problems have been dealt with, as the use of other mind-altering drugs will not help them to control their approach to alcohol. Perhaps the most important group to exclude, however, are those whose problem drinking has led to physical illness and who would be wise to avoid any further damage from alcohol.

A plus factor for clients being assessed for involvement in normal drinking treatment is a positive desire to aim for such a goal. Often, though, problem drinkers have attempted for many years to control their drinking and know better than anyone that they cannot do it. If clients resolutely request an abstinence goal, it would be destructive in the extreme to convince them otherwise. Besides, for a client to return successfully to normal drinking, family and social network support are essential.

Assessment must look at these factors closely and examine all the other areas of the client's personal and social life which may mitigate against the attainment of normal drinking habits.

Techniques useful in attainment of normal drinking
Letting the client set the agenda is a sound rule for nurses working with clients whose therapeutic goal is normal drinking. In this way, the programme ultimately designed is one with which the client can identify, and one to which the client will have a high level of commitment.

Identification of dangerous situations
As a first step, the nurse/therapist should identify the situations in which the client feels it is difficult to control drinking patterns. Initially, it is wiser for clients either to avoid such occasions or to maintain an abstinence rule in those circumstances. Often clients are very inventive and imaginative in identifying their own strategies and neutralising the dangerous situation. For example, a woman at home who finds the afternoon boring and particularly prone to the onset of uncontrolled drinking may decide to fill that time with other activities such as keep-fit classes or further education.

The beverage – quantity and frequency
Particular drinks have strong associations for problem drinkers. If in the past the 'treatment' for social anxiety has always been an excess of whisky, then it might make the goal of normal drinking easier to change to a beverage that has not previously been used in that manner. Nurses must recognise that it is not simply a matter of alcoholic content; the actual nature of the drink means much more than that to the client, and something as simple as having a glass of wine or beer when they would normally have chosen their favourite drink will help with control.

In addition, the nurse will need to agree with the client the desired frequency and the measures allowed for drinks. People pouring their drinks at home rarely measure them in the way publicans do, and some objective measure agreeable to the nurse and client should be arrived at.

Sipping, not gulping
There is a huge body of evidence that problem drinkers drink at a noticeably faster rate than their peers. It is useful to make clients aware of this and to get them to 'pace' their drinking, either against the company they drink with or against the clock, by making one drink last an agreed time.

Close monitoring of progress
Any attempt by a client to achieve the goal of normal drinking must be closely assessed and monitored. It is a difficult time, lasting months if not years, and the client will need to be seen at regular intervals to discuss successes and failures. The programme must remain totally flexible and open to renegotiation at any time if the client finds it difficult. It is of the greatest importance that the client (and not simply

the therapist) should be committed to this goal of treatment; it takes much therapeutic strength and insight to recognise that an approach in which the therapist has invested a great deal is not right for a particular individual. For the sake of clients we must also develop the skills to know when we are wrong.

Women and drug/alcohol problems

Women are increasingly experimenting with illegal drugs. However, it remains the case that, throughout this and the previous century, women's drug problems have centred on the abuse of prescribed drugs and alcohol. Gomberg (1982) outlines the link between the opiate-based products sold by the travelling medicine man and the corner shop in the nineteenth century, to the massive usage of psychoactive drugs by women in the twentieth century. Women are not only bigger users of psychoactive drugs; they are, perhaps more importantly, much more likely to be prescribed psychoactive drugs than men. There is some evidence that where men are forced through unemployment to adopt 'female' carer roles in the home, their use of psychoactive drugs on prescription also increases.

Gender and the use of drugs for medicinal and therapeutic purposes have a very strong link which cannot be satisfactorily explained by anatomy. There are definite physiological stages in a woman's life (menstruation, pregnancy, childbirth, lactation and menopause) when hormonal or emotional changes, or negative feelings about the process stemming from strong cultural mythology, can mean that women turn to drugs to lift moods or alleviate anxiety at these particular times.

The clear physical markers in a woman's life are often also accompanied by a change of role. Oakley (1974) claims that:

'the two themes which underlie the continuing social differentiation of women from men are domesticity as a defining feature of the women's situation, and ambivalence in the cultural values applied to women's roles. Since the social stereotype of women portrays them as domesticated, a view of women as people is always mixed with a perception of their social difference from men: they are housewives.'

These differences in sexually assigned roles and the ambivalence that surrounds women may provide us with some clues to the 'rules' that underpin women's drug and alcohol use. Women work traditionally in caring for others; husband, children, elderly relatives. Any substance use that would render the woman incapable of performing this sustaining role is viewed by society as extremely threatening. Man's traditional social role lies outside the home, and does not involve any responsibility, in a direct sense, for the welfare of others. As Gomberg (1982) points out, 'the care of a field can be postponed for a day; the care of a child cannot'. Oakley (1974) makes the same point in a somewhat more forceful manner.

> 'As a consequence of industrialisation, the home means 'family' rather than 'work'. Our language contains the phrase 'a family man', but there is no corresponding phrase for women. It would be socially redundant: the family *means* women.'

With women as social carers, their drug and alcohol use may be looked at as an attempt to escape the tedium of a life at home devoid of any stimulating adult company. Or, perhaps, for the woman who has since early childhood been socialised to care rather than be cared for, entering the 'sick role' via dependency on drugs or alcohol is one way of seeking to have her needs for care fulfilled, if not by others, at least by her own 'medicine'.

The social ambivalence about women's roles extends to society's attitude towards women drinking. Vast amounts of the advertising industry's efforts now go towards encouraging women to drink more and more, with a fair measure of success. Additionally, the retail outlets for alcohol have mushroomed and women are now able to buy alcohol quite easily as part of the normal household shopping. Public houses and other licensed establishments go out of their way to 'feminise' their premises in an attempt to attract female customers in larger numbers. In contrast to these now well-established trends, it is still considered wrong for a woman to drink to excess. Not only is this view connected with the caring, nurturing role of women – 'the hand that rocks the cradle is not supposed to have a drink in it' – but moreover female intoxication has always been associated, from Biblical times, with sexual looseness and availability. It could be argued that controlling and curtailing the manner of female drinking is also about controlling and curtailing the free experience of female sexuality.

Issues in treatment

Women problem drinkers or drug takers are different from men, both in terms of social roles and personal needs. It is essential that the specific issues about being a woman in this society are understood by those planning treatment responses. Women historically underuse facilities open to both men and women, and tend to be attributed a poorer prognosis when they do use them (Birchmore and Walderman 1975). Treatment facilities in both drug and alcohol inpatient settings were designed for male clients, who at one time would have made up over 90% of the clientele.

Women have been admitted to these services and to counselling services without, in the main, any major adjustments to treatment approaches. Page (1980) claims that the most important factor in treatment is how an alcoholic woman views herself and the changes she needs to make to her self-image. Crucial to this process will be the attitude of treatment agencies and helpers involved with her. Women drinkers and drug takers often have very low levels of self-esteem and see themselves as powerless and inadequate. Nurses engaged in counselling must fully come to terms with their own views of women's drinking and drug taking, or they will not be able to enter the therapeutic alliance in a constructive way.

Group work and women

Group work of a therapeutic nature has long been the traditional method of treatment in most inpatient settings. The objective of group work is to provide a safe, facilitated, supportive environment in which group members can, by identifying with each other, examine intrapsychic conflicts and in time come to terms with themselves and their problems. Whilst many male substance abusers do well in these treatment settings, there is some evidence that women find it difficult to become part of a mixed sex group or to find the friendship and *bonhomie* which seems to be a therapeutic factor for male clients. Page (1980) cites a study of group interactions at Scalebar Park Alcohol Unit. It was noted that newly admitted female clients were more able to talk freely about their problems and feelings in a weekly women's only group, whilst in the mixed sex group they tended to defer to male group members, or to enter once more the role of supporter and carer. There are obvious implications for treatment agencies wishing to serve the needs of women more effectively:

1 *Accessibility of services* – crèche and family support services; appointments made realistic for women with small children.
2 *A separate treatment forum* – room for women to be able to examine their own issues before looking at their feelings about men and relationship difficulties.
3 *Sensitivity to the problems* – nursing staff must become more aware of how treatment approaches simply mirror the dominant value system within society. They must become more aware of their own feelings about women and dependency.

Drugs, alcohol and elderly people

The increasing heroin problem in the early 1980s and the very necessary initiatives in the care of drug users have firmly focused concern on the young opiate user. This has been recently reinforced by the AIDS threat to those who inject drugs, once again making this group very important in terms of political responses and the provision of services.

Whilst these young drug users are obviously a vital group to target, their very 'visible' social behaviour and the illegal nature of their drug use often serve to promote the impression that they constitute the largest drug problem for society. Recent research, however, proves otherwise (Plant *et al.* 1985). One of the major issues concerning the use of drugs by young people is the massive investment we place in our children, both as a society and as individuals. Any threat (real or perceived) to their future well-being is, quite rightly, taken very seriously; but because of their tremendous social worth, such a threat is given unwarranted importance.

Quite the opposite happens, however, when it comes to the elderly, amongst whom drug abuse constitutes a much larger and at times equally destructive social problem. In a society which seems to have struck the words 'death' and 'dying' from its vocabulary and refers instead to 'passing away' or 'falling asleep', and which avoids when possible all reference to old age, it is hardly surprising that a major problem of drug and alcohol abuse among the elderly should be, in the main, ignored or denied. The fact is that old people use more drugs than any other age group; in the majority of cases, this drug use falls into three main categories:

1   Prescribed drugs.
2   'Over the counter' drugs.
3   Alcohol.

Eckhard (1978) specifically cited 'over the counter' drugs as a problem, with the finding that per-capita expenditure on drugs was four times higher among the over-65s. Another American study by Chien *et al.* (1978) also found extensive use, in particular of analgesic drugs among the over-60s.

Although these and other studies were conducted in the US, their conclusions are supported by the few research studies carried out in the UK. In 1975, Carlson pointed out that the elderly, who at the time constituted 12% of the population, consumed over 30% of the total NHS spending on drugs (Carlson 1975). There is evidence that since that time longer life expectancy has led to an increase in the number of people classed as elderly, and a parallel rise in prescribing practices. Of course, one of the reasons why the elderly are prescribed (and consume) more drugs is that they suffer from multiple pathology; conditions such as heart disease, rheumatism, blood pressure abnormalities and chronic chest conditions all require frequent medication. However, evidence from a study in England by Malcolm (1984) suggests that the problems of polypharmacy in the elderly are not simply a response to multiple pathology; in a sample of 223 patients with an average age of 77, Malcolm found that all of them took an average of 2.9 drugs per day, whilst over a third of the sample took 4 or more different drugs each day. Interestingly, the vast majority of these drugs were not of the type one would expect to be prescribed in response to the usual conditions of ageing, but rather they were often psychotropic drugs prescribed to alleviate or mask the social and psychological problems posed by the elderly.

These social and psychological problems are a common accompaniment to the physical disabilities associated with old age. Society, in treating the aged as a very undervalued commodity, creates a situation in which many of them feel (often realistically) that they are sitting around waiting for death. Loss of loved ones, economic uncertainty, forced retirement and social isolation all combine with poor physical health to produce depression, anxiety and sleeplessness. In Malcolm's study (1984), 35% of patients were prescribed benzodiazepines, 33% phenothiazines and 15% antidepressants. These findings suggest that doctors are prescribing to compensate for the lack of other facilities that would more appropriately fill the void in many elderly people's lives.

Drug misuse by the elderly takes four main forms:

1 Overuse.
2 Underuse.
3 Erratic use.
4 Contraindicated use.

The potential for the elderly to encounter unwanted effects from medication is greater than for younger people; a study by Crome (1982) in Oxford found that adverse drug effects accounted for at least 15% of admissions to geriatric wards. When drugs are prescribed, it is generally assumed that the prescribing instructions will be complied with. Among the elderly, however, non-compliance is the rule rather than the exception and is directly related to the number of drugs prescribed: compliance becomes much less likely when more drugs are prescribed and their dosage becomes more complex.

A finding common to most studies of drug misuse in the elderly is the usually undiagnosed and often denied problem of alcohol abuse: Malcolm (1984) found that 1 in 10 of the elderly people in his study clearly suffered from this problem, and that there was a surprisingly high denial of any alcohol consumption. Similarly, Mishara and Kastenbaum (1980) suggest that 6% of the elderly population have an alcohol problem. Elderly drinkers are either 'remote onset', i.e. have had a drinking problem for a long time in adult life and have continued in old age, or 'recent onset' in response to the pressures of old age. This latter group is more likely to go unnoticed.

It is therefore difficult to estimate just how many of the elderly population have a significant drink problem, as most of them do not seek or receive help for a number of reasons. Shame, guilt and denial mean that the problem remains hidden, often with the collusion of friends and relatives who supply the alcohol. The stigma of alcoholism is felt most acutely by the elderly, exacerbating their feelings of shame

and loss of self-esteem. Furthermore, friends, relatives and professionals often add to the problem with attitudes expressed in such
statements as 'Why shouldn't they have a drink or two at their age?' and
'Well, they are going to die soon, so why shouldn't they get drunk if they
want to?' These 'opinions' do not take into consideration the mental
and physical effects of alcohol abuse on the elderly and can only help to
worsen the quality of life for those whose old age could otherwise have
been a pleasant experience. When hospitalisation does occur as a result
of alcohol abuse, health workers are often reluctant to recognise the
drink problem, either through ignorance or through age prejudice,
treating instead only the accompanying physical effects, and unwilling
to 'waste' – as they see it – time and money on therapy for someone
'who will die soon anyway'.

It is now recognised that elderly problem drinkers need and respond
to specialised treatment plans that combine generalised care of the
elderly with an emphasis on their alcohol consumption and its resulting
problems.

Weatherill (1987) has outlined a treatment strategy for an elderly
problem drinker (this plan could be easily modified for use with an
elderly person abusing prescribed medication).

1 Assessment of the client's condition

Mental: memory loss, confusion, signs of dementia, etc.
Physical: anaemia, signs of poor nutrition, other age-related illnesses,
etc.
Environmental: lives alone or with others, home conditions, need for
sheltered housing? etc.
Psychosocial: isolation, contact with family/friends/others, finances,
etc.

2 History from the client
Including the time of onset of problem drinking, how they feel about it
and about themselves, and quantity and frequency of alcohol intake.

3 History from relatives/significant others
This is important, as the client often underestimates the extent of the
problem.

4 Establish the role of relatives/significant others
Collusion – do they supply alcohol for the patient? Do they have
feelings of guilt, anger, shame?

5 Establish the need for education of relatives/significant others
Education may be needed to deal with their feelings towards the

problem drinker and the role alcohol has to play in the present problem (they can be referred to the weekly relative support group meeting held at the hospital).

6 Formulate short-term treatment goals
Does the client need detoxification, and if so, as an inpatient or outpatient? As there are often alcohol-related physical problems, the inpatient solution is usually preferable since it offers the opportunity to assess in full the physical and mental state of clients as well as their ability to look after themselves.

What other agencies need to be involved in the client's future care? The general practitioner may not be fully aware of the situation and would probably have to be contacted; so should the district nurse, health visitor, 'meals on wheels', the social services (if bath, toilet and home aids are likely to be needed) and community psychiatric nurse specialising in alcoholism, if possible.

7 Long-term plans
Consider the further involvement of outside agencies such as Home Help, Good Neighbour schemes, day centres, etc.

8 The use of a key worker
This is essential to liaise and coordinate the care of the client with all the community workers. Many agencies may need education on problem drinking and drug taking.

Other treatment
In conjunction with the physical, environmental and sociological care offered, a weekly open-ended therapy group exclusively for elderly problem drinkers may prove useful. These groups can be immensely valuable in providing the opportunity for participants to talk about the feelings, fears and frustrations that have led to their overuse of alcohol. In addition, the support and education clients receive within the group may have a positive influence on their future behaviour.

Not all elderly problem drinkers will comply with the treatment offered. This should not exclude them from the care of community agencies, but rather it means that treatment may have to be on a day-to-day basis, dealing with situations of risk as they occur, and intervening whenever necessary or appropriate. As with all elderly people, their pride and reluctance to accept help have to be respected, which explains why the role of the key worker is of paramount importance in establishing a more personal, less clinical relationship with the problem drinker, taking the time necessary to develop the trust required for the elderly person to discuss his or her problems.

The nurse working with the elderly should recognise the failure of society to accept that the old person has the same desires, feelings and requirements as the young. Indeed, as Simone de Beauvoir (1970) points out, to accept the elderly problem substance abuser means to recognise that old people 'still retain the virtues and the faults of the men (and women) they were and still are'.

AIDS and injecting drug misuse

Injecting drug use has always been a risky activity, in the physical and social sense. Users are subject to a whole host of health-damaging factors every time they inject illegal drugs. It is common for street drugs such as heroin and cocaine to vary in strength and quality. The dangerous practice of 'cutting' (mixing the drug with a substance of similar appearance in order to increase profits) the drug with other sedatives or minor tranquillisers is not uncommon, and leaves the user open to the ever-present danger of overdose.

Usually the substances used by dealers to 'cut' street drugs, such as talcum powder, are not dangerous in themselves but cause enormous problems when injected into the bloodstream and surrounding tissues, setting up irritation and infection leading to blockages in the venous system. In minor cases, this will show as nothing more than a nasty ulcer which refuses to heal; in more severe cases, the user risks amputation or death.

Transmissible diseases such as hepatitis B and infective endocarditis are common among injecting drug users. Robertson (1987) claims that the levels of hepatitis B infection in this category may be as high as 85%, many of them remaining asymptomatic or writing off mild malaise as the norm.

Along with the inherent dangers of injecting adulterated and possibly impure street drugs, there is the hazardous lifestyle resulting from illegal drug misuse in individuals without the means to support their habit. Thus most illegal drug users neglect their diet, which explains the somewhat stereotyped image of the gaunt, painfully thin injecting user. This failure to ensure adequate, balanced nutrition leads in turn to other physical problems, such as skin infections, constipation, vitamin deficiency, a general malaise and predisposition to recurrent infections.

Injecting drug users without a very high personal income must develop a lifestyle aimed at financing their habit. This involves them in enormous social and legal risks every day; those who manage to maintain a job risk censure and dismissal, whilst others who must steal or prostitute themselves live in a world in which violence is common, and the chance of either arrest by the police or being placed in danger by peers or clients remains an everyday experience.

Any discussion of work with injecting drug users in relation to the dangers of AIDS must start from a recognition of this inherent riskiness in their lifestyle. It is against this background that the particular problems posed by the growing spread of the AIDS virus must be faced. Injecting drug users are now the second largest group of HIV infected individuals after gay men (outside Africa). Estimates drawn up by the Centre for Disease Control show that up to 20% of all AIDS cases in the USA and as many as 50% in some specific areas are injecting drug users. In the UK, Edinburgh finds itself in the devastating position of having 50% of its injecting drug users testing positively for HIV. This percentage represents up to 2000 injecting users, without counting the consequences for their sexual partners and children, as already reported by Brettle *et al.* (1988). In other areas of the UK, the picture is not yet so clear or devastating, but, as Skidmore (1987) suggests, we should not be too optimistic as this may simply stem from a lack of research resources in unreported areas rather than the absence of the virus.

In response to the threat of an epidemic, attempts have been made to encourage drug misusers to change their ways. The government has launched health education campaigns aimed primarily at them, in much the same way that the gay community was once targeted. Alongside these national approaches, local drug agencies, drug problem teams, drug dependency units, etc., are faced with the day-to-day issue of adapting (often longstanding) methods in response to AIDS. Many of these agencies have adopted a drug-free, no maintenance prescribing, abstinence approach for decades, and they have seen generations of problem drug users prosper as a result of their intervention, precisely because this methodology proved right for them. It is with great trepidation that most of these agencies now listen to the 'new wisdom' in the dependency field, which seems to insist that they become involved with everything they have eschewed for years. In the USA, particularly in New York and New Jersey, they have been struggling with these problems for some time as services became inundated with AIDS cases. By 5 January 1987, there were 2914 cases of AIDS among heterosexual injecting drug users in New York state and 785 in New Jersey, whilst there were only 1411 in the rest of the USA. Des Jarlais (1988) has documented the effects produced by AIDS on drug services in New York, and claims that responses can be identified as distinct stages with enormous implications for the therapeutic responses of clinical workers.

The first stage is *denial*. Staff working with problem drug users continue to operate as before and tend to deny the importance of HIV. Des Jarlais notes two particular aspects of this phase of denial. The association of AIDS with death constitutes a definite obstacle to drug treatment, in which the building up of hope for a better, brighter future is often an important factor. Another vital issue raised by AIDS is the need to acknowledge the very high level of relapse among injecting drug users. In the past, nurses and others have often been able to avoid talking about what possible failure (i.e. a return to injecting) might entail; now, possible failure also means possible death, and in counselling the client on the dangers of relapse, the nurse must acknowledge it as a very real possibility. Des Jarlais (1988): 'To discuss AIDS with a patient in treatment raises the possibility of treatment failure'.

Denial is followed by *panic*. Even when it is no longer possible to deny the existence of AIDS and HIV in the drug field, evidence from New York does not suggest that it is easy to deal with. Clinical workers' responses bordered on panic, characterised by a thirst for information on AIDS. Even in the face of conclusive evidence about the absolute lack of any danger of transmission from casual contact, Des Jarlais found that agency staff frequently handling bodily fluids for analysis or living in treatment settings were subject to widespread fears about transmission of the virus. These fears sometimes resulted in the infected person being transferred or somehow removed from treatment. In order to 'get through' the panic phase, staff needed to be able to express fears, receive support and develop guidelines for new ways of working. If this was achieved, workers progressed to the next phase; if not, the continuing fears and consequent scapegoating of clients was likely to worsen.

The third stage of *coping* involves the ability to incorporate AIDS issues into the everyday treatment of drug misuse. The workers functioning at this level see the prevention of HIV transmission and AIDS as an integral part of their clinical role. In the case of users who are not in contact with treatment agencies, prevention needs to be diverse and may not necessarily entail the elimination of injecting drug use; approaches such as syringe and needle exchange schemes, education about safer sexual practices, the importance of general health measures and diet in relation to the immune system, advice on safer injecting practices and the availability of maintenance prescribing will all be vital in helping them cope with the danger of AIDS in the drug abusing community. However, it is not simply a matter of clean syringes; drug misusers are not like the gay community who tend to be better integrated into the mainstream society – often well educated, working in responsible jobs and with high disposable incomes. Any campaign aimed at drug misusers must take into account their hazardous lifestyle, as well as their lower social and economic status.

It would be very sad indeed if the current need to emphasise prevention of AIDS and HIV infection before the prevention of injecting drug misuse was merely an expression of therapeutic nihilism in the difficult field of drug misuse, rather than a clearly thought-out combination of responses. The conflict many workers feel about the changes towards 'risk reduction' rather than 'treatment' is heightened by the all-or-nothing approach to these changes in the UK. It is not unusual to see services once geared to a treatment model or counselling method change within a few months into a maintenance service and syringe exchange facility. Unfortunately, all too often these speedy shifts in orientation are not based on any real theoretical understanding and take place without a full discussion of all the issues involved, including a thorough working out of the fears and concerns of staff. In a sense, these rapid changes in the face of AIDS could be seen as an unhealthy resolution of the 'panic' phase, as they do not contain the necessary elements to make it a healthy process, as Des Jarlais argues: 'Working through the panic stage involves not only written communications and formal training, but also staff meetings, the rumour network within programmes, and interpersonal confrontations'.

In many ways, a quick turnabout of services from one exclusive orientation to another is not all that useful, and could be seen as essentially ducking the real issue, i.e. we need not a winding down of drug treatment services but an expansion. As the Royal College of Psychiatrists (1987) points out, the first factor in this expansion must be the prevention of drug misuse, followed by an increased effort to discourage injecting and sharing needles, as well as help and comfort for the infected or sick drug users.

The need for the development of drug services is all the more urgent in the light of the growing number of AIDS cases in which injecting drug misuse was the primary source behaviour. Des Jarlais and Friedman (1987) point out that in September 1984, injecting drug misuse was the primary risk behaviour in only 2% of known AIDS cases; by September 1986, this stood at 13%. They report:

> 'Once HIV becomes established among intravenous drug misusers in a local area, drug use becomes a primary source for heterosexual and *in-utero* transmission . . . Control of the AIDS epidemic in the United States and Europe will thus require control of HIV infection among intravenous drug users.'

The Department of Health has identified five major objectives in their campaign aimed at drug misusers:

1 To reduce as far as possible any experimentation with drugs and especially to prevent experimentation by injecting.
2 To persuade those who will not stop using drugs, that they must abandon injection and use a safe method of administration.
3 To persuade those who will not stop injecting to use sterile, non-shared equipment, and hygienic injection practices.
4 To provide all possible encouragement and support to help individuals to stop drug misuse or to prolong periods of remission from misuse.

5   To educate all misusers about the extent of the risk of spreading the virus to their heterosexual partners.

In order to advance towards *all* of these objectives, we require trained specialists who understand the nature of drug misuse and have at their disposal an armoury of interventions solidly grounded in theoretical understanding. If this does not happen, the danger is that in response to the AIDS threat, nurses will abandon any real attempt at therapeutic intervention and simply become the dispensers of clean syringes. Nurses working in the drug field must move from the 'panic' stage to the 'coping' one. To quote Des Jarlais (1987) once again:

> 'The great need to prevent further HIV transmission, and the realisation that the surest way to prevent needle-sharing transmission is to stop drug injecting, override any potential conflict between providing AIDS education and the treatment goal of eliminating illicit drug injection.'

REFERENCES

Birchmore D. F., Walderman R. L. (1975). The women alcoholics: a review. *Ontario Psychologist*, 7 (4), 10.

Brettle R. P., Bisset K., Burns S. *et al.* (1987). Human immunodeficiency virus and drug misuse: the Edinburgh experience. *British Medical Journal*, 295, 421–3.

Carlson R. I. (1975). *The End of Medicine.* New York: John Wiley.

Chien C., Townsend E. J., Townsend A. R. (1978). Substance use and abuse among the community elderly: the medical aspect. *Addictive Diseases*, 3 (3), 357–72.

Crome P. (1982). Drug compliance in the elderly. In *Psychopharmacology of Old Age.* Oxford: OUP, pp. 55–64.

De Beauvoir S. (1970). *Old Age.* Harmondsworth: Penguin.

Des Jarlais D. C. (1988). Stages in response of the drug abuse treatment systems to the AIDS epidemic in New York. In press. *Journal of Drug Issues.*

Des Jarlais D. C., Friedman S. R. (1987). HIV infection among intravenous drug users: epidemiology and risk reduction. *AIDS*, I, 67–76.

Eckardt M. J. (1978). Consequences of alcohol and other drug use in the aged. In *Biology of Ageing* (Behnke J. A., Finch C. E., Gardner B., eds). New York: Plenum Press.

Edwards G. (1982). *The Treatment of Drinking Problems.* Oxford: Blackwell.

Gomberg E. S. (1982). Historical and political perspective of women and drug use. *Journal of Social Issues*, 38, 9–23.

Hobson R. (1986). *Forms of Feeling: The Heart of Psychotherapy.* London: Tavistock.

Kaufman E., Kaufman P. N. (1979). *Family Therapy of Drug and Alcohol Abuse.* New York: Garndner Press Inc.

Malcolm M. T. (1984). Alcohol and drug use in the elderly visited at home. *International Journal of Addictions*, 19 (4), 411–18.

Mishara B. L., Kastenbaum R. (1980). *Alcohol and Old Age*. New York: Grune and Stratton.

Nelson-Jones R. (1983). *Practical Counselling Skills*. London: Holt Saunders.

Oakley A. (1974). *A Housewife*. Harmondsworth: Penguin.

Page A. (1980). *Counselling in Women and Alcohol*. London: Tavistock.

Plant M. A., Peck D. F., Samuel E. (1985). *Alcohol, Drugs and School Leavers*. London: Tavistock.

Robertson R. (1987). *Heroin, AIDS and Society*. London: Hodder and Stoughton.

Rogers C. (1951). *Client Centred Therapy: Its Current Practice, Implications and theory*. Constable.

Rollnick S. (1985). The value of a cognitive–behavioural approach in the treatment of problem drinkers. In *The Misuse of Alcohol: Crucial Issues in Dependence, Treatment and Prevention*. (Heather N., Robertson I., Davies P., eds), Beckenham: Croom Helm.

Royal College of Psychiatrists (1987). *Drug Scenes*. Gaskell.

Skidmore C. (1987). AIDS and intravenous drug users. *Health Education Journal*, **46**, 2.

Weatherill J. (1989). Unpublished paper.

Chapter 6

The role of the non-specialist nurse

This chapter outlines the areas of concern for nurses working in a non-specialist capacity in three different environments: the community, the hospital and the workplace. It is important that nurses working in a specific environment do not see their role in isolation. Nurses in a community setting have much to learn about management of people who are intoxicated from nurses who work in an accident and emergency department. For each of these non-specialist nurses, examples are given of what are considered to be appropriate areas of intervention. It is important that nurses consider their role outside of that immediate environment, and ensure that the information they obtain is accurate, up-to-date and non-stigmatising.

THE COMMUNITY

The community is one of the most important areas for detecting and managing people with substance abuse problems. Nurses in this area play a major part in ensuring that clients and their families are given the opportunity to explore the difficulties associated with the misuse of substances.

Interventions in a community setting can often be based upon an early judgement that 'all is not well', but one must carefully consider the costs and benefits of such intervention. The dividing line between a 'wait and see' strategy and passive collusion is not great.

We consider here the role of community psychiatric nurses, district nurses, health visitors and school nurses.

The community psychiatric nurse (CPN)

Later in this chapter we describe the 'dual problem' syndrome, i.e. clients with a psychiatric illness whose misuse of substances is closely linked to such presentations. An awareness of this is required by psychiatric nurses in the community who must be alert to the coping mechanisms of their clients, whether a 25-year-old woman with postnatal depression or a 60-year-old man with a longstanding history of mental illness. The possibility of these clients using drugs or alcohol as a form of self-medication is great, especially as the perceived effects are often stimulation and symptom relief. As many large psychiatric hospitals close, the importance of adequate formal and informal structures for former residents cannot be emphasised too greatly, and in the absence of easily accessible (both in terms of locality and opening hours) social networks, the likelihood of alcohol being used to ease social interactions is considerable. Community psychiatric nurses must continue to provide support and where appropriate act as advocates for these vulnerable clients.

The use of drugs including minor tranquillisers is often reinforced by calendars from the manufacturers displaying peaceful scenes in the surgery! Catalan *et al.* (1984) looked at the effects of non-prescribing of anxiolytics in general practice. In their study, 91 patients with new episodes of minor affective disorders were selected by their general practitioners as suitable for anxiolytic medication. Half the group were allocated randomly to a 'drug group' (i.e. prescribed anxiolytic) and half received brief counselling without anxiolytics. Each intervention was measured one month and seven months later; improvement in psychiatric state and social function were similar and parallel in the two groups. It is noteworthy that the non-drug group did not make increased demands on the doctors' time. This is an example of the kind of work that community psychiatric nurses have the skills and knowledge to develop.

One of the dilemmas that nurses in this setting face is that they are encouraging some clients to take and maintain their intake of medication, whilst at the same time discouraging others. This may play a part in the ambivalence that nurses experience when dealing with substance abusers, which is sometimes reflected in a resistance to using the specialist services in a consultative capacity, preferring to refer clients to them for 'treatment and management'. Such an approach can have the effect of clients perceiving themselves as an unpopular 'parcel', faced by a confusing range of services. The generic CPN has many of the skills which are based within the principles of counselling, thus enabling the client with problems associated with the misuse of substances to be cared for in a familiar and relatively safe environment.

The provision of advice by the CPN as part of a general assessment of the client's use of alcohol or drugs as a means of coping with distress, anxiety or pain, may well enable the client to share the concern about such behaviour with the CPN. We recommend that the taking of a full drug and alcohol history be part of the routine assessment protocol of any CPN.

CPNs are well placed to provide a central role in the development of such strategies as home detoxification and family therapy, as well as being a valuable link with local self-help groups and community groups. Because of the wide range of contacts that these nurses have (directly with clients and indirectly with the community at large), they are in a position to warn about substance misuse long before it becomes a major problem.

The district nurse

District nurses usually care for the sick in their own homes giving basic nursing care such as blanket bathing, injections and dressings. Because of their wide range of responsibilities, district nurses encounter patients at different stages in their illness, and therefore can play a critical role in the recognition and treatment of problems associated with substance abuse.

Whilst research has given us some estimate of the percentage of substance abusers who contact hospital-based services, literature about contact with non-specialist community nurses is scant. Shaw *et al.* (1978) looked at the reasons why there is a limited response by non-specialist community agents to problem drinkers. They highlighted the following reasons:

1 Anxieties about role adequacy through not having the information and skills necessary to recognise and respond to drinkers.
2 Anxieties about role legitimacy, through being uncertain as to whether (or how far) drinking problems came within their responsibilities.
3 Anxieties about role support through having nowhere to turn to for help and advice when they were unsure how to respond.

These problems are not unique to the district nurse but are highlighted in their role. District nurses are primarily there to care for the physical needs of these patients, yet if somebody is drinking heavily or using drugs, it is impossible and unprofessional to ignore this behaviour. It is likely that they may be asked for advice by relatives or neighbours who have started purchasing the substances because the person is unable to leave their home (it is not unknown for off-licences in London to make 'home deliveries' for people who are physically unable to get to them). In addition to their other work, district nurses should find the time to clarify with their clients what role substances are playing in their lives. Drinking and drug histories should be integrated into the routine nursing assessment, and a good knowledge of local services is essential.

It is understandable that a community nurse might be ambivalent about considering whether a patient has a drug or alcohol problem; but ignoring warning signs or obvious symptoms will only suggest to the client that either the behaviour is acceptable, or the nurse is blind!

The health visitor

Health visitors hold a unique position in the health service, being mainly concerned with the prevention of illness. They work alongside other members of the health care team, as health educators and advisors, both in the home and in the health centre. Contact with the family occurs most often after the birth of a baby, when the health visitor commences home visiting to advise on child care. Responsibilities also include teaching principles of healthy living to mothers, children and the elderly. By implication, a major goal is to reduce the risks of ill-health in vulnerable groups through prevention. Health visitors will encounter large numbers of people affected by substance abuse, either as users themselves or as relatives of users. Having regular and systematic contact with these families gives repeated opportunities to review use of substances.

Case history

Sheila is 26 and had her first child three months ago. The health visitor has seen her every few weeks to review progress and has noted that the flat is sparsely furnished and cold. This does not fit with the initial assessment, when Sheila volunteered that she is living with Des, who is a successful clothes manufacturer. Further discussion with Sheila revealed that Des has been injecting heroin for the past six months, and she feels the child may be the reason why.

This case highlights many of the problems encountered by health visitors, although the substance of abuse may differ. It is important to decide where the priorities lie. Is it to ensure that Sheila and her child are given as much help as possible (whilst being certain that Des does not spend all the money), or is it to try to help Des? The answer is not clear cut. The immediate priority is to be certain that Sheila and the child are not at risk, and in the longer term to see how accessible Des is to help. At this juncture, it would be appropriate to have discussions with the local specialist service and arrange a home visit with them. In essence the prime aims should be:

1 The adaptive handling of the immediate stress so that it does not precipitate family disintegration.
2 The development of responses that enable the family to handle the situation in the future.
3 The re-establishment of a stable, healthy family equilibrium or lifestyle.

Health visitors also have a responsibility for ensuring that adequate health education is given during the preconception and prenatal period. Accurate, non-judgemental information should be provided (see section on the role of the midwife or obstetric nurse, p.127).

The school nurse

The experimental and recreational use of drugs has often been thought of as a school-based activity. The young person's exposure to drugs increases with age, as does the choice of available substances. Plant *et al.* (1984) report from a study of drinking habits and alcohol-related consequences amongst 1036 Scottish teenagers. This study revealed that, for both males and females, serious alcohol-related consequences were significantly correlated with tobacco consumption and with the use of illicit drugs. These results support the existing evidence indicating that multiple use is commonplace amongst young people.

The student is unlikely to come to the attention of the school nurse because of a substance abuse problem. It is often as a consequence of such use (e.g. poor attendance, feeling unwell and falling asleep in class, increased frequency of accidents) that a student is seen, and it is therefore essential that the school nurse develops a high index of suspicion in order to determine what is happening to the student. Careful history taking and looking for symptoms of substance abuse should assist this. It is worth noting that drugs may be obtained not just from fellow students but by looking in the medicine cabinets of their parents. Parents and children need accurate information to make a sensible and informed decision about their use or non-use of substances. Such decision-making is best developed by exploring how students make other decisions. Scare tactics are not likely to work: wheeling in an ex-drug addict or problem drinker will have little, if any, effect. Students cannot identify with these people, as they have not reached that stage of misuse. Students usually know very little about drugs, and to provide them with this information is a much more realistic and sensible approach.

This has been highlighted by the American Academy of Pediatrics who outlined the following objectives:

1   Educate paediatricians how to interview, identify, counsel and manage young people (and their families) who are using drugs, including alcohol. This objective should be extended to include education of paediatric residents and medical students.

2   Become actively involved in the support and implementation of comprehensive educational programmes for children, young people, their families and the community regarding drug or alcohol use, in consort with liaison groups already engaged in that activity.

THE HOSPITAL

Nurses in several hospital environments encounter people who are there owing to their use of drugs and/or alcohol. Amongst these are nurses in general wards, accident and emergency departments, obstetrics and general psychiatric wards.

The general nurse

A considerable amount of research has looked at the extent of alcohol problems amongst admissions to general hospitals. In 1982 Barrison *et al.* examined all patients admitted to Charing Cross Hospital in London over a two-week period. By using a questionnaire that combined items on alcohol consumption with the four CAGE questions (see below), it was discovered that 15.6% to 23.2% of patients were classified as abnormal drinkers. Abnormal drinkers were defined as men who admitted to regular consumption of more than eight units of alcohol per day or women who drank more than four units of alcohol per day. In addition, the CAGE questions were used to define abnormal drinkers, a positive response to two or more questions indicating an abnormal attitude to drinking. The questions are:

1 Have you ever thought you should Cut down on your drinking?
2 Have you ever been Annoyed by criticism of your drinking?
3 Have you ever felt Guilty about your drinking?
4 Do you drink in the morning (do you have an Eye opener)?

The questions on consumption alone detected 95% of the abnormal drinkers, the largest proportion of whom were in emergency surgical, orthopaedic, psychiatric or general wards (see Table 6.1).

Nurses in these settings have an opportunity to develop such skills and by detecting the person, can assist in their early referral for advice and necessary treatment. The rationale for this type of minimal and yet effective intervention is highlighted even more by Chick (1985). Having identified 156 men admitted to medical wards as problem drinkers, he then allocated them to one of two groups. One group received a session of counselling about their drinking habits from a nurse, and the other received routine care. At twelve month follow-up both groups reported a reduction in consumption, but the counselled group had a significantly better outcome than the control group. Two rather different case studies help to illustrate the point.

Case history 1

Mr Thomas has been admitted via the medical outpatients department. He is 38 and is suffering from liver damage. He has been admitted on six occasions in the last two and a half years. The liver problems are caused

Table 6.1 *Proportion of 'abnormal' drinkers in each speciality (Barrison* et al. *1982)*

Speciality	Period I		Period II	
	Low estimate	High estimate	Low estimate	High estimate
	%	%	%	%
Emergency medicine	20.0	42.1	9.1	10.0
Routine medicine	14.8	27.5	11.1	16.6
Emergency surgery	27.7	75.0	41.1	51.8
Routine surgery	17.2	26.3	21.1	26.6
Orthopaedics	16.3	24.2	24.0	31.6
Psychiatry	18.7	25.0	22.2	25.2
Genitourinary surgery	10.9	19.2	12.5	16.6
ENT/dental/ ophthalmology	4.7	12.0	19.5	24.2
Gynaecology	0	0	10.0	12.5
Overall prevalence of 'abnormal' drinking	15.6	20.2	23.2	26.9

by his heavy drinking. When advised by the staff nurse that he should abstain from alcohol, he says, 'Why should I? What have I got to gain? The drink helps to keep the pain away.'

Case history 2

Helen is 23 and has been admitted through the accident and emergency department early on Monday morning with acute gastritis. On admission, she is intoxicated but once sober, several hours later, she acknowledges that she had too much to drink. The nursing staff outline the possible consequences of continuous use of alcohol, and after some consideration she agrees to see somebody from Drinkwatchers about controlling her drinking.

No doubt Mr Thomas was admitted many years ago because of a similar specific bout of heavy drinking, and had the nurses talked to him then as they did to Helen, the outcome might have been very different.

Whilst research has not been focused upon these techniques with problem drug users, the principle of early detection and referral for treatment and advice still prevails. It is sometimes assumed that the drug user will be more easily detected, but this is not necessarily the case. Withdrawal symptoms may be mistaken for a bout of influenza, and restlessness is often treated by the prescribing of hypnotics, thus masking the withdrawal symptoms. Drug users may present in a wide range of ways, including (as a result of overdoses) respiratory problems and convulsions. The medical hazards of injecting can lead to admission to hospital with abscesses, thrombophlebitis, gangrene, septicaemia or hepatitis B. The appropriate control of infection precautions should be taken during this time. Nurses will need to use the time that a drug user is in hospital effectively. Once the immediate physical problems begin to subside, drug users want to be on their way; information and advice should therefore be targeted within the first few days of admission.

The accident and emergency nurse

The intoxicant effects of drugs and alcohol increase the likelihood not just of medical disorders but also of accidents. The opportunities for nurses in these environments are immense and could provide the forum for considerable preventative strategies. To start with, we should recognise that many of these people may be intoxicated and by implication require nursing intervention.

Management of intoxicated clients

Clients who are intoxicated can present in several ways. When someone is intoxicated to the level of unconsciousness, adequate support should be given to ensure that physiological function is maintained. Investigations to determine the cause of unconsciousness should be initiated, which should include speaking to friends, relatives and neighbours who may be able to set the scene.

The clients that cause the most concern are those whose intoxicated behaviour is disruptive. An analysis of such behaviour may help to understand how to manage disruptive behaviour more effectively. This can be completed by identifying the behaviours that cause problems, the situations in which they occur, examining what actions staff take in response to these behaviours, and identifying the behaviours that are preferred (Fig.6.1).

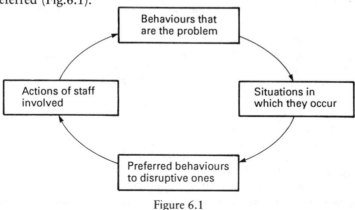

Figure 6.1

The type of strategy used will be determined by the client's behaviour, the staff judgement of the seriousness of the disruption, departmental procedures for back-up, and staff skill and experience. Staff can help to reduce undesirable behaviour by routinely identifying the clients concerned, what they do and, if necessary, the approximate time involved in the completion of treatment in the department. Avoid asking too many questions at one time, since this may only confuse and anger. Speak with self-assurance and make clear by your communication that you control the situation.

Contingency contracting is a useful method for management of disruptive behaviour. The contract is a specific and clear statement of the behaviours that are to be increased and decreased. It describes for the individual when the desirable or undesirable behaviours occur. The contract should be specific, firm, fair, reasonable and positive. All staff in the department must be consistent in the implementation of the contract.

Case history

Jane comes to the accident and emergency department almost every Friday night. Her level of intoxication varies but the demands are the same. She is dependent upon dihydrocodeine tartrate (DF 118), after being given them for a short period following a Pott's fracture. Whilst intoxicated by alcohol her demands are for DF 118. Friday nights are usually the busiest and in the past, for the sake of a quiet life, some medical and nursing staff have acceded to Jane's demands. An analysis of this situation reveals that the staff involved are usually the juniors and the regular time of Jane's arrival is about midnight. Whilst staff feel negative about Jane, attention is usually focused upon her as she is a familiar figure. When the attention moves away to somebody else, she becomes increasingly demanding until such time as she is seen. Even though prescribing of DF 118 is now very rare, it is Jane's behaviour that is causing the problems.

After discussion amongst the team, a strategy is agreed. It is recognised that Jane finds the contact with the staff to be a positive experience, so the following is decided:

1 Jane will see the *same* member of the team on each visit. All communication will be through this person – a senior staff nurse.
2 Disruptive behaviour by Jane will be ignored, and if necessary she will be asked to leave.
3 Consistent and specific advice about the services for people with drug problems will be provided.

Advice to accident and emergency attenders

As drugs and alcohol may be an influence in attendance at the department, advice and information should be available. Sometimes the drug users or abnormal drinkers are obvious, or present with a very distinct medical problem. However, many of the attenders may have 'cleared their heads' by the time they get to hospital. In 1987 University College Hospital in London developed the role of a nurse specialist in drug and alcohol problems, with responsibility for assessing and providing information for those people who present in the accident and emergency department with a suspected drug or alcohol problem. This kind of work could be achieved on a more modest scale locally, by appointing one or two team members to acquire further knowledge and experience, and this can ensure an effective service to what is often a hidden client group.

The midwife or obstetric nurse

The role of substances such as drugs, alcohol and cigarettes in the development of the fetus evokes very emotive feelings. As a result nurses often feel ambivalent about caring for mothers with substance abuse problems. The opportunity should be provided to explore these feelings, rather than dealing with them by being angry towards the patient. Care is outlined in the antenatal and postnatal periods.

Antenatal period

Planned pregnancies provide a valuable focus for the midwife and obstetric nurse. Providing information and advice can help clients to make informed decisions. Stortz (1977) recommends a comprehensive integration of drug information in antenatal counselling. Such information needs to be given in a non-judgemental way which maintains the client's self-esteem and decision-making ability. If an expectant mother is considered to be at risk, early referral to the local treatment service is advised.

There continues to be tremendous controversy about the advice that should be given on alcohol consumption in pregnancy. The following statement from the US Surgeon General (1981) is emphatic:

'Even if she does not bear a child with full fetal alcohol syndrome, a woman who drinks heavily is more likely to bear a child with one or more of the defects included in the syndrome. Microcephaly, which is associated with mental impairment, is one of the more common of these defects. The reported defects on pregnancy outcome appear to be independent of potentially confounding variables, including nutrition and smoking. Each patient should be told about the risk of alcohol consumption during pregnancy and advised not to drink alcoholic beverages and to become aware of the alcoholic content of foods and drugs.'

Tylden (1983) strongly advises that a fertile woman wanting to conceive should come off drugs before she stops contraception.

However, as opiates can cause amenorrhoea, pregnancy may come as a complete surprise. Early withdrawal from the drug through hospital admission is recommended, otherwise the fetus may show a fetal withdrawal syndrome. Withdrawal must not be allowed to progress to the stage of muscle cramps, because true fetal distress can then occur, with the possibility of premature labour.

Postnatal period

The fetal alcohol syndrome is due to excessive maternal consumption of alcohol, especially during the first trimester. There is a variable range of symptoms, which include gross retardation, mental retardation, neurological dysfunctions and congenital abnormalities. In the first few days following birth, the baby may exhibit withdrawal symptoms which will require urgent medical intervention. Any baby whose mother has been abusing opiates, tranquillisers, hypnotics, benzodiazepines or analgesics can develop an abstinence syndrome. Such babies may be underweight and remain irritable for several months after birth.

If during pregnancy or labour it is evident that the mother has a drug or alcohol problem, contact should be made with the local treatment services. There is a strong likelihood that the mother will feel bad enough about her substance abuse without encountering the wrath of others. However, a very careful social and psychological assessment has to be made in collaboration with the local social services department as to what is the best intervention for mother and baby (Table 6.2). As Phillips (1986) says:

> 'If midwives in clinics do not welcome addicted mothers and facilitate their attendance by a caring attitude and warm, flexible approach, the women will miss out on antenatal education and monitoring. It is essential for the atmosphere to be non-judgemental with perhaps a liberal appointment system if the client is to cope with the hassle of the clinic's structure.'

The psychiatric nurse

The details on the type of intervention that can be developed by psychiatric nurses is outlined elsewhere in this book, but it is appropriate to address a few areas in particular. These include the management of clients who have a psychiatric illness and use substances to deal with this, and the care and treatment of patients experiencing Wernicke's encephalopathy or Korsakoff's psychosis.

Psychiatric illness

In the study by Barrison *et al.* (1982) between 18.7% and 25.2% of clients in psychiatric wards were defined as abnormal drinkers. Usually,

Table 6.2

Type of drug	Treatment in pregnancy	Treatment in labour
Heroin, morphine, methadone and other opiates	Slow withdrawal of the drug is necessary, and oestriols should be monitored. Fetal irritability can occur in acute withdrawal which can lead to intrauterine death	Mother needs an opiate in labour to prevent fetal distress, as well as routine analgesia/anaesthesia
Barbiturates (eight times the therapeutic dose and greater)	Substitute a barbiturate with a long half-life, i.e. phenobarbitone, during withdrawal to prevent fits	Phenobarbitone cover in labour plus an ordinary analgesic
Phenothiazines	Small doses seem safe, and can be given during pregnancy	Potentiates normal analgesia
Benzodiazepines	Use drugs with a long half-life during withdrawal	Watch the fetus
Psychedelics	Stop the addict taking them and give phenothiazines symptomatically	Watch the BP and pulse rate of the mother, who may need phenothiazines
Amphetamines	Stop the addict taking them	Routine treatment
Cocaine	Stop the addict taking it	Routine treatment

we think of the client who has been admitted for detoxification, rather than the depressed patient who may use alcohol or opiates as a form of self-medication.

Case history

Jonathan was admitted to the acute admission ward, with a history of a depressive illness of two years' duration. This had been preceded by the sudden death of his wife. They had been married for fifty years. Because he was agitated, Jonathan had been prescribed some antidepressant drugs. Having been in hospital for six weeks, he began to take weekend leave and the depression got worse rather than better. This continued for several more weeks until a student asked Jonathan about his use of alcohol, and found that at weekends he was drinking half a bottle of spirits to cope with loneliness.

In the case of Jonathan, no drinking history was taken on admission. Yet Bernardt *et al.* (1984) found that by using a screening interview a nurse could obtain an accurate drinking history from psychiatric patients.

Similarly, patients may be admitted in a manic or psychotic state which is drug-induced. There is always the possibility that some underlying psychological problems stimulate substance abuse. Bakdash (1987) correctly describes this as a 'chicken and egg dilemma' and goes on to suggest the dual problem (of substance and psychiatric illness) as a cyclical process (Fig. 6.2). An assessment of all psychiatric patients on the basis of this model should assist not just in identifying the possible use of substances but also the coping mechanisms that need developing.

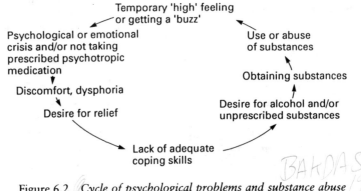

Figure 6.2 *Cycle of psychological problems and substance abuse* (by permission of John Wiley & Sons Inc.)

Wernicke's encephalopathy, Korsakoff's psychosis

Wernicke's encephalopathy and Korsakoff's psychosis are complications of the central nervous system resulting from thiamine deficiency. Such conditions are rare, but are associated with a history of chronic excessive drinking, poor eating habits and poor absorption of nutrients. Liver problems can also affect the metabolism of thiamine. However, Price and Kerr (1985) report a high incidence in Australia; an examination of patients with the syndrome in a Queensland mental hospital revealed an excess of those who had undergone partial gastrectomy, and also an excess of single males and widowers. They conclude that consumption of beer does not explain the situation and suggests that lifestyle factors (e.g. social isolation) are likely to be of greater importance.

The acute symptoms are mental confusion and excitement in conjunction with peripheral neuropathy. This is usually followed by more severe deterioration of memory, including confabulation and loss of capacity to judge what is true.

Vitamin replacement and a highly nutritious diet may assist in the management. The client will require a considerable amount of patience in helping them to relearn certain skills that ensure an improvement in the quality of their life. Careful assessment of occupational skills is required in order to assist rehabilitation.

THE WORKPLACE

Many people who misuse drugs or alcohol are in regular employment. Specialist services tend to see clients who are unemployed, probably because many of their clients have a longstanding history and are referred late in their career of substance abuse; also some services provide a Monday to Friday, 9.00 a.m. to 5.00 p.m. service, which in itself limits the access of clients who are working.

The nurse in the workplace plays a major role in assisting employers in meeting the health and safety needs of their employees. An alert occupational health nurse needs to be aware not just of the problems that the misuse of drugs or alcohol may cause for the employee, but also of the possible risks to the safety of other employees, and in some situations, to the consumers of the service. Malloy (1983) argues that health assessments can provide a good opportunity for the nurse to observe any sign that a person may have an alcohol problem. The cost of such problems to the employer may be considerable, through loss of efficiency, absenteeism and accidents associated with drugs or alcohol consumption. There are varying estimates of such costs in financial terms, and one study (McDonnell and Maynard 1985) states that the cost in sickness and absence associated with alcohol in England is £641.51 million.

General studies

The majority of researchers have reviewed the extent of alcohol problems in the workplace; problems associated with the misuse of drugs – including tranquillisers – have gained little attention. The biographical characteristics of 334 patients were reviewed in 15 ATUs in England and Wales in 1973 (Hore and Smith); the most common occupational groups presenting were seamen, public house workers, hotel and restaurant workers, nurses, medical practitioners and company directors. A specific examination of some occupational groups by three Austrian researchers found the incidence of liver damage amongst brewery workers to be much higher than two comparable groups and concluded 'heavy drinking for the brewery worker carries no financial burden; consequently, he has the opportunity to imbibe limitless quantities of beer'. Plant (1979) also found that employment in the brewing and distillery industry was associated with much higher levels of alcohol consumption, and as time progressed, greater levels of alcohol-related problems. Rose and Glatt (1961) found amongst seamen that pressure to drink and possible predisposition to alcohol problems were the main factor.

Case history

Mike was 52 when he presented to the community alcohol team. Having worked for 27 years in the Merchant Navy, he had spent the last 9 years odd-jobbing, and when referred was employed as a chef in a large hotel. The welfare officer had given him a written warning as he had been late for work several times and she felt that this was because of his drinking.

Because of his many years in the Navy, Mike's perception of social drinking was inaccurate. Until he was 18 he was not allowed any alcohol, but once he had reached that age the 'tot' of rum was provided. Mike worked in the galley, and was eventually promoted from handling the vegetables to handling the meat. This meant he had to frequent the freezer more often, and so his alcohol intake increased ('the rum keeps you warm,' his superior told him); thus began a pattern of increased consumption as his responsibilities changed. Because of this very gradual development, Mike was able to integrate the increase into a 'normal' pattern and this played a role in his misperception.

Roman and Trice (1970) felt that amongst company directors, problem drinking may be actively concealed or even fostered by ambitious subordinates.

Stimson *et al.* (1984) noted the extent of drug abuse in the medical profession, although they looked only at information kept by the Drugs Branch of the Home Office. Such doctors were most often discovered through police activity (they had been convicted of drug offences) and appeared on disciplinary charges before the General Medical Council.

From a review of the main areas of study, the following points are worth noting. Firstly, the eight factors identified by Plant (1979) as influencing the incidence of alcohol problems in the workplace:

1 The availability of alcohol.
2 Social pressure to drink.
3 Separation from normal social or sexual relationships.
4 Freedom from supervision.
5 Very high or low income.
6 Collusion by colleagues.
7 Strains, stresses and hazards.
8 Preselection of 'high-risk' people.

Secondly, an examination of the liver cirrhosis mortality rates according to occupational group (see Table 3.9 on p. 65).

Nurses with drug or alcohol problems

The incidence of substance abuse amongst the nursing profession is of great concern. Unfitness on duty due to alcohol and/or the misappropriation of drugs was noted as cause for concern in the General Nursing Council of England and Wales annual report for 1978/9. In the year 1980/1, there was a 61% increase of alcohol or drug-related cases compared to 1977/8 (Kennedy 1984). The problem is not unique to England and Wales, and in the United States a considerable amount of progress has been achieved. It is difficult to determine the extent of the problem. Often the basis of the statistics is the number of nurses who have to attend an investigating body: yet, because the problem is often covered up, it is likely that these nurses represent the tip of a very large iceberg. Bissell and Jones (1981) estimate that there are about 40 000 alcohol-dependent nurses in the United States; and in the study of 100 alcohol-dependent nurses, they found that most of the nurses had been in the top third of their class, held advanced degrees, were in demanding and responsible jobs, and were highly respected for excellent work that continued long after they began to drink – clearly not fitting the stereotypical image of drunken nurses. The message from nurses who themselves have experienced problems is clear (Talmadge-Reed 1986):

'The subjects overwhelmingly emphasised the need for education about the incidence and course of chemical dependence. Many said that nurses need to know it is not a moral issue, but a treatable illness. The subjects felt that nurses need to be educated about the incidence of illness in their own profession and need to learn to support and help one another. As one subject summed up, "the only wrong thing to do is to do nothing for the chemically dependent nurse" .'

The nursing profession has long been seen as a credible area of activity, yet nursing rarely if ever brings to view in a sympathetic way colleagues with alcohol or drug problems. The basis of this group collusion is not clear; perhaps admitting to human weakness might be seen as questioning our professional identity. Little could be further from the truth. The practice of some nurse managers (from ward sister to chief nursing officer) of 'waiting and seeing' until the time a patient or nurse becomes vulnerable is intolerable and inhumane. The extent of alcohol and drug problems in the profession clearly indicates that all is not well, but a more proactive than reactive approach is required. The nurse who colludes or ignores a situation is just as (if not more) responsible for the consequences than the nurse with the problem. Similarly, a manager who chooses to use a 'sledgehammer' approach to deal with a sensitive personal problem has a lot to answer for.

Students with drug or alcohol problems

Nurses in educational settings, whether as tutors in schools or lecturers in university, are very likely to encounter students whose use of drugs or alcohol worries them. Such transitions as the move away from home and the stress of developing new social networks mean that some drugs (and alcohol in particular) are used to smooth the edges of social interaction. Waring *et al.* (1984) found considerable differences between the patterns of alcohol use by graduate students in social work and business. Irrespective of previous course work or work experience with alcoholics, social work students wanted alcohol education, whilst business students had a 'blind spot'. This kind of work has implications for teachers or vocational counsellors in these settings. Amongst first-year medical students, increased communication from significant others and interpersonal support correlated with reduced student drinking during the first twelve weeks of medical school (Gardner *et al.* 1983).

Indicators of drug or alcohol problems in the workplace

The problem drug user or drinker in the workplace may be defined as an employee whose consumption of drugs or alcohol repeatedly or frequently affects work performance or normal adjustment to work. There are four main categories that may point to such a problem.

1   Work performance – lower productivity, spasmodic work pace, poor concentration and quality of work, and a high level of mistakes and errors.
2   Absenteeism – increased frequency of days off, repeated absence on first and last days of the week, increased minor illnesses.
3   Changes in behaviour and personality – neglect of detail, tendency to blame others for shortcomings, sensitivity to reference about drinking, intolerant and verbose.
4   Accidents – frequent injuries, increased time off, careless handling, lack of safety sense.

The response

One response is to collude with the problem, in other words turning a blind eye or taking action to prevent accidents being caused (e.g. transferring the employee to other work). This approach solves little. The worker will probably maintain the consumption of the substance, and will represent a loss to the organisation in respect of efficiency. Secondly, the employee may be dismissed, especially if there is a deterioration in work performance. Although this may solve the immediate problem and have a slight salutary effect on the employee concerned, it represents to the organisation a loss of investment in that person's training. A more positive and beneficial approach is to encourage employees who have problems to seek assistance and treatment. If employees work in an environment that is not hostile to them and where the problems that arise are understood, they are more likely to acknowledge their problems and volunteer for treatment. This process can be helped by developing an employment policy in the workplace.

The objective of the employment policy should be to assist employees in the interest of health and safety at work, by setting out the organisation's intentions with regard to confidentiality, job security, sickness benefits, pension rights and disciplinary procedures. The major principles of the policy should include:

1 Assistance in obtaining advice and help would be given, including time off.
2 Employees who come to the attention of management through accidents, work deterioration or drug or alcohol-related problems would be given the opportunity to discuss their problems.
3 Employees would be encouraged to seek help voluntarily.
4 Protection of pension rights and benefits while in treatment would be provided.
5 Refusal of diagnosis or help, or discontinuation of a recovery programme, will not in themselves be grounds for disciplinary action, but continued unacceptable behaviour and standards of work will be dealt with through normal disciplinary procedures.
6 The treatment record will be kept confidential.
7 Employees would have the right to be represented by their union at any stage.
8 The policy is common to all employees, irrespective of grade and status.

An employment policy is not worth the paper it is written on unless the organisation is committed to its implementation. Discussions should include management, occupational health personnel and trade unions. Once a policy has been agreed, a method of publicity (possibly via pay packets) and a system of evaluation should be incorporated.

REFERENCES

Bakdash D. (1987). Psychiatric/mental health nursing. In *Substance Abuse* (Bennett G., Vourakis C., Woolf, eds) New York: John Wiley, 223–39.

Barrison I. G., Viola L., Mumford J., Murray R. M., Gordon M., Murray-Lyon I. M. (1982). Detecting excessive drinking among admissions to a general hospital. *Health Trends.* 14, 82–3.

Bernardt M. W., Mumford J., Murray R. M. (1984). Can accurate drinking histories be obtained from psychiatric patients by a nurse conducting screening interviews. *British Journal of Addiction*, 79, 201–6.

Bissell L., Jones R. W. (1981). The alcoholic nurse. *Nursing Outlook*, 29 (2), 96–101.

Booth P. G., Gillard G. (1981). Nurses with drinking problems. *Nursing Times*, 1676–8.

Catalan J., Gath D., Edmonds G., Ennis J. (1984). The effect of non-prescribing of anxiolytics in general practice. *British Journal of Psychiatry*, 144, 593–602.

Chick J., Lloyd G., Crombie E. (1985). Counselling problem drinkers in a medical ward: a controlled study. *British Medical Journal*, 290, 965–7.

Gardner R., Wilshack S. C., Slotnick H. B. (1983). Communication, social support and alcohol use in first year medical students. *Journal of Studies on Alcohol*, 44 (1), 188–93.

Hore B., Smith E. (1973). *Who Goes to Alcoholic Units*. Paper presented at Institute for Prevention and Treatment of Alcoholism. Belgrade.

Kennedy J. (1984). Wanted – a policy for problem staff. *Nursing Mirror*, 159 (6), 9.

McDonnell R., Maynard A. (1985). The costs of alcohol misuse. *British Journal of Addiction*, 80, 27–35.

Malloy J. (1983). Alcohol and the occupational health role. *Occupational Health*, 447–53.

Phillips K. (1986). Neonatal drug addicts. *Nursing Times*, 19 March, 36–8.

Plant M. A. (1979). *Drinking Careers: Occupations, Drinking Habits and Drinking Problems*. London: Tavistock.

Plant M. A., Peck D. F., Stuart R. (1984). The correlates of serious alcohol related consequences and illicit drug use amongst a cohort of Scottish teenagers. *British Journal of Addiction*, 79, 197–200.

Price J., Kerr R. (1985). Some observations of the Wernicke-Korsakoff syndrome in Australia. *British Journal of Addiction*, 80, 69–76.

Roman R. M., Trice H. M. (1970). The development of deviant drinking; occupational risk factors. *Archives of Environmental Health*, 2, 424–35.

Rose H. K., Glatt M. M. (1961). A study of alcoholism as an occupational hazard of merchant seamen. *Journal of Mental Science*, 107, 18–30.

Shaw S., Cartwright A., Spratley T., Harwin J. (1978). *Responding to Drinking Problems*. London: Croom Helm.

Stimson G. V., Oppenheimer E., Stimson C. A. (1984). Drug abuse in the medical profession: addict doctors and the Home Office. *British Journal of Addiction*, 79, 395–402.

Stortz L. J. (1977). Unprescribed drug products and pregnancy. *Journal of Obstetric, Gynaecologic and Neonatal Nursing*, 6 (4), 9–13.

Talmadge Reed M. (1986). Descriptive study of chemically dependent nurses. In *Readings in Psychiatric Nursing Research* (Brooking J. ed). Chichester: John Wiley.

Tylden E. (1983). Care of the pregnant drug addict. *MIMS Magazine*, 1 June.

US Surgeon General (1981). Advisory on Alcohol and Pregnancy. *FDA Drug Bulletin*, **1** (2), 29–100.

Waring M. L., Petraglia G., Cohen L., Busby E. (1984). Alcohol use patterns of graduate students in social work and in business. *Journal of Studies on Alcohol*, **45** (3), 268–71.

Chapter 7

Prevention of substance abuse and its problems

It is essential when discussing preventative measures to ask first what may appear to be a rhetorical question: what exactly do we mean by prevention? It is a term used extensively throughout the helping professions, especially nursing, as if everyone involved in the debate had the same understanding of its meaning. When we examine the term, and also the manner in which it is used, it becomes clear that 'prevention' can be applied to a whole range of activities, objectives and outcomes. For many nurses, particularly those working in the community, prevention has always been seen in terms of the three-stage model as follows:

1 *Primary prevention*: preventing substance abuse problems from starting in the first place.
2 *Secondary prevention*: any substance abuse problems that do occur are spotted early and prevented from developing.
3 *Tertiary prevention*: once the problem has developed, intervention is aimed at responding to it and preventing further damaging consequences.

Tether and Robinson (1986) argue that although this division is a logical and tidy way of dealing with prevention in the literature, it presents many problems when put into practice in the substance abuse field. They point out that agencies in the field often have the capacity to respond to clients' problems at all three levels in an approach combining assessment, intervention and evaluation. Artificial divisions between the various levels of prevention may only serve as a model and have little practical use when working with clients.

The Advisory Council on the Misuse of Drugs, in its report *Prevention* (DHSS 1984), also rejected this three-stage model of prevention on the grounds that it was not sufficiently comprehensive to cover all elements of prevention policy. Instead, the Council adopted an approach to prevention satisfying two basic criteria: (a) reducing the risk of an individual engaging in drug misuse, and (b) reducing the harm associated with drug misuse. The latter criterion allowed preventative strategies in the drug abuse field to move for the first time in a legitimate manner towards developing approaches aimed at 'risk reduction' in dealing with those for whom 'stopping' was not on the agenda.

Another way of viewing the concept of prevention is to identify the focus of intervention. What is the major focus of our attention? The answer will depend largely on the individual's personal and professional belief system about the causes of substance abuse. For example, if the professional worker dealing with problem drinkers believes that problems with drinking are a result of special features (physical or psychological) of their clients, then the prevention strategies employed by that worker will be orientated to change the client in some way. If, on the other hand, the nurse takes a more sociological or environmental view of the causes of substance abuse, then strategies for prevention will be aimed at changing or manipulating the client's environment. A third focus for many experts in the field lies in the substances themselves. Prevention, it is argued, can only be achieved by controlling access to the substances concerned. Whilst this is an objective of most governments in relation to illegal substances, it does not constitute an option that politicians are willing to consider when it comes to legal drugs such as alcohol and tobacco. Not only would such a measure be politically unpopular and financially costly, it has historically proved impossible to implement and would simply displace legal drugs into the category of illegal drugs.

Prevention, then, is by no means an easy concept, and becomes more difficult when applied to substances that millions of people enjoy. Although there is a notable lack of consensus in the literature on what constitutes prevention, as Davies (1985) points out, 'Prevention, like mother love, is something that few people would doubt to be of positive value'.

In posing the question of what exactly constitutes prevention, we must distinguish three ways in which the word is used:

1 *Stopping* – prevention in its absolute sense means 'to stop' or 'to keep from coming to pass'. Applied to the substance abuse field, this use of the term would be aimed at eradicating any occurrence of problems.

2 *Hindering* – prevention can also mean 'to hinder', to make it more difficult for the problems that are the focus of the preventative action to come about. Unlike 'stopping', this interpretation of prevention is not aimed at necessarily reducing the frequency to zero.

3 *Curtailing* – prevention is also used in the sense of 'curtailing the

progress of'. Whilst similar to hindering, it is usually used in the sense of preventing increases of a present problem – maintaining it at its existing level.

Not only do we have difficulty in determining what we mean by prevention, we also suffer from confusion when asked to define what it is we are attempting to prevent. There is, throughout most preventative approaches, an unhelpful tendency to lump together all substance-related consequences and behaviour as though they shared the same antecedents and were amenable to the same sort of therapeutic intervention. Any nurse working with individual clients knows that this is a grave danger. Clients use substances and abuse them for a host of reasons, but there is a common factor that most generalised prevention strategies miss – that people who use substances do so because they believe or perceive them to have benefits. This use or abuse continues often in full knowledge of the costs, because the overriding belief of the individual is that the benefits outweigh the costs.

Health education concepts

It is interesting to examine the various approaches to health education that have consistently been used in the substance abuse field, mostly with little success. The major thrust of health education is rooted firmly in an educational model. The idea is that if you give people sensible, factual information that something is bad for their health, then they will absorb this information and the consequence will be a change in behaviour. This model presumes a link between knowledge, attitudes and behaviour which is tenuous to say the least, and for which there is relatively little evidence. As Dorn (1987) points out, attitudes to mind-altering substances are linked in all manner of ways with image, status in a peer group, and emotional and situational contexts. Using a model of alcohol abuse or alcohol-related problems, it is possible to illustrate that aiming preventative strategies at health-related problems such as intoxication, liver disease and alcohol poisoning, all directly the consequences of drinking alcohol, do not in any way address the context and interaction-related consequences, as well as the perceived benefits of alcohol.

There is another problem particular to alcohol. Preventative health education in this sphere suffers from an ambivalence and ambiguity not evident in any other field. The messages are mixed. On the one hand, some people are potentially or actually having problems as a result of too much drinking; the message for these people is that alcohol is a bad substance which must be stopped or limited. However, other messages lead to the idea that a little will actually do you good. This ambivalence, combined with the tremendous amounts spent by the drinks industry on the positive message, is one of the major reasons for the ineffectiveness of most campaigns.

The reader may at this point be led to ask: what about smoking? Surely health education in relation to the ill effects of smoking has been effective? Certainly the decrease in the number of adults smoking (mainly males) is encouraging, and the plea for people to 'look after themselves' has had positive effects.

Smoking, however, is somewhat different from alcohol in a health education context, for a number of reasons. The 'disease concept' of problem drinking and the deviant model of drug taking means that the public can conveniently ignore messages based on an 'us and them' level. It is easy to return to the theory of disease or deviance and regard the messages about alcohol and drugs as being for 'them' not 'us'. In the case of smoking this is not so easily done, as there is no well developed and widely known disease concept of smoking; and so the public find the messages more applicable to them and thus more difficult to ignore. Perhaps of even more importance is the strength of a campaign that only has one message, i.e. smoking is bad for you, all cigarettes are damaging to your health, there is nothing positive about them. The strength of this message, combined with changes in the public's attitudes to health and a growing awareness of taking action for themselves, has led to success in convincing many people to stop smoking.

It is also important to realise that prevention is made more complex by the aetiology of substance abuse. Plant *et al.* (1985) draw our attention to this factor and claim that effective prevention strategies will have to be based on sensitive analyses of cultural realities rather than on any reflex formulation, and that often multiple strategies will be needed.

Preventative action in the field of substance abuse can be considered on three levels.

National level

Intervention at national level covers the political initiatives and the mass media campaigns. Unfortunately, because national prevention campaigns are 'high profile' and very visible to the electorate, they are usually opted for before a sufficient investigation into either their need or effect has been carried out. Often – all too often – they are not founded on a sound data base, and evaluation remains minimal. Experts involved closely in health education call for more integration of national policies with treatment facilities. It is nonsense to mount a high-level campaign such as the government's anti-heroin campaign in 1986, if the people targeted by the campaign (slogan 'heroin really does screw you up'), have to stay that way because of lack of treatment facilities! What Thorley (1985) refers to as the link between politics and propaganda, however, remains difficult for government ministers to resist. The mistake of funding a huge, high-profile media advertising campaign, before any counsellors on the ground existed or were trained, has been repeated in the case of AIDS. According to Plant *et al.* (1985), it would be more useful for national prevention planning to be aimed at encouraging and integrating local action.

When nurses are involved in top-level government decision making, it is difficult to see where they might have a role at this level of preventative action. However, nurses are employed at the DHSS to advise ministers on just these issues and to report (via the English National Board and the UKCC) the concerns of the profession. Also, nurses who are concerned that national initiatives in prevention are outstripping resources on the ground, have the right of every citizen to let the profession and the politicians know of our concern.

International level

On an international level, preventative action in relation to substance abuse tends to concentrate mainly on the problems of illicit drug use. There are now well-developed means at the disposal of various customs, police, or other law enforcement agencies. The development of technological support for these agencies and the increased willingness to share information all help to form the basis of a coordinated international strategy. A major segment of the international strategy of prevention is aimed at financially wooing the poor farmers in opium or coca growing areas of the world to grow a different crop. The general principle behind this policy is that the richer Western nations who face huge problems of illicit drugs being sold in their countries will give cash incentives to producing countries to tempt peasant farmers away from those crops. Although this sort of international initiative has had limited success, the fact that the illicit drugs market can pay well for their crop, the inaccessibility of some of the areas concerned and the involvement of gangster methods militate against effective long-term results.

Local level

Nurses are more likely to be professionally involved with prevention at a local, personal level. In the past decade, following experience in the United States, the focus of preventative action has swung firmly in favour of localised 'user friendly' services which should, when possible, be demystified, 'debureaucratised' and fully open to community involvement.

The vital task of involving local members of a community in preventative action may be more and more the work of nurses in primary health care teams or specialist substance abuse teams. Plant *et al.* (1985) point out that there exists at local level a multiplicity of organisations that can be utilised in a preventative strategy;

organisations such as community centres, groups, schools, youth clubs, colleges, religious organisations and women's groups form part of the infrastructure of any local community. Members of these organisations are often ideally placed to monitor substance abuse levels and the need for specific action within their community. In many cases, because of special relationships with members of the community (not always enjoyed by the visiting health care professional) members of these organisations will be able to mobilise resources to provide help, in the form of support networks or counselling groups for people in trouble with particular substances. Any nurse wanting an example of the power of self-help in the dependency arena need look no further than Alcoholics Anonymous; it is (despite its somewhat dubious beliefs about causes of problem drinking) a fine example of what can be achieved by the sort of commitment not possible from professional workers.

Community groups can also monitor and often control the availability, and inhibit the supply of, certain substances within the local area. This they often do in full cooperation with the police, who do not usually have the same information that is open to people of particular standing within the community.

The success of such localised initiatives in the USA when they have been combined with specific 'on the ground', effective and cognitive-based education campaigns have proved superior to traditional high profile campaigns. Previous attempts to raise young people's awareness of the possible problems of substance abuse have usually been based on 'scare tactics', designed to frighten people away from the substance. Messages are normally couched in the idiom of 'thou shalt not' and 'this is a bad substance', usually followed by warnings of the awful grief that awaits anyone who ignores the original message. All these scare campaigns manage to achieve is a reaffirmation of the already existing stereotypes, often making it easier for people to place themselves in a different camp and therefore to shut off the message.

These approaches to health education are dogged by enormous problems and contradictions, all well documented but, it would seem, easy for politicians to ignore. The basis of the fear model is that if an extreme emotion such as fear is aroused by a communication, associated recommendations for changes in behaviour will be followed in order to achieve a reduction in the arousal level. However, as Stacey (1981) vividly points out, the communication may in fact fail to 'scare', fail to evoke the necessary emotional response. Even more importantly, should the recommended action leave residual fear, then the subject will ultimately be more likely to ignore the message totally. Perhaps in the context of a debate about dependency, one could point out the dangers for those who get high on fear!

Other problems with fear-based health education stem from the enormous difficulty of appealing to people to behave in a way that is socially defined as 'good', or in their best interests, or in the interests of the community. As we have pointed out earlier, the problem is that the individual substance user or abuser may not perceive things in quite the same way. Reference must also be made to the hypocritical nature of the message, in that alcohol and drugs are freely available and in fact 'pushed', not by the stereotyped pusher on the streets, but by big business at all levels of politics and economics. To expect the person using or abusing these substances to ignore all the social and cultural influences that led to that involvement would indeed be extremely foolish.

More effective approaches

In many instances, substance abuse education is moving towards a more person-centred, holistic approach. Emphasis is placed not on the substance and on simply giving information, but on a 'whole person health model' as opposed to the 'bad substance, sick model'. These moves have developed from a number of philosophical bases.

The public health approach
The focus of this approach is the interaction between the individual, drugs and the environment (Fig.7.1). These three elements overlap and interact constantly, with many drugs having a potential for abuse or the production of dependency. Thus, involvement or non-involvement with a particular drug will often be dependent on a number of sociological variables.

The psychosocial approach
This model places emphasis on the subjective meanings that individuals obtain from their chosen substance and the 'scene' that surrounds it. The rewards gained by the individual from using the substance constitute the focus of this model. This approach outlines two major types of expectation:

1   Young people live in a society that actively promotes the use of a variety of recreational drugs and views it as a normal adjunct of 'adult' behaviour, even going so far as to suggest in its promotion of these substances that they actually enhance our 'adultness'. It should not then come as much of a surprise that for many young people, growing up and assuming an adult role may also involve using a variety of recreational and medicinal drugs.
2   Substance misuse is also seen by this model as a means of coping with stress and attempting to solve problems imposed by society.

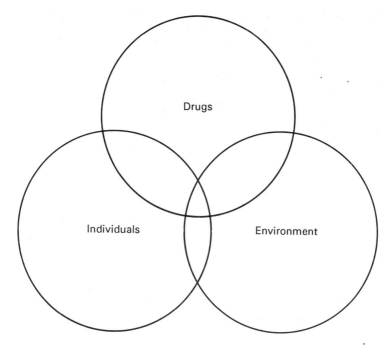

Figure 7.1

The structural approach

Health educators are becoming increasingly aware that in order to understand substance abuse and to develop effective preventative strategies, we must take into account the importance of the social and cultural context in which the substance is used. This model attempts to analyse the norms and behaviour developed by specific social sub-groups as a response to their position in the social and economic structure. Such factors as social class, lack of life chances, poor housing, lack of upward social mobility and inequality in health provision are all seen as structural factors, often quite outside the control of the individual, although they remain the major determinants of people's lives.

Cognitive/affective health education

Providing simple, factual information about substance abuse without examining, in a sensitive way, the cognitive and affective factors attached to it not only does not deter young people from experimentation, it is claimed, but increases their curiosity and possibly their tendency to experiment. Using a cognitive and affective approach, health educators aim to assist individuals to make informed decisions about using certain substances. Williams and Vejnoska (19??) cite the usefulness of this approach when incorporated into an holistic approach to health and the individual:

> 'The body is conceptualised as a wonderful piece of machinery that, like an automobile, has a limited lifespan. With proper and periodic maintenance, exercise, good habits and identified limitations, the body like the car can be very responsive.'

A similar emphasis is placed on mental and emotional well-being, and the importance of developing social and coping skills such as clear values, a positive self-image, sound decision-making skills and stress management or coping mechanisms.

The overall aim is to assist the individual in building skills that will be useful at times of social pressure – including pressure to use or abuse substances.

Media campaigns and programmes for action

Many questions have been asked – and almost everyone in the dependency field has an opinion – about the effectiveness of high-profile media campaigns. It might be useful to examine briefly two well-documented, high-profile campaigns dealing with different substances.

Thorley (1985) discusses the difficulties of the media campaigns that took place in the northeast of England between 1974 and 1979. Although these were part of a major national initiative on alcohol education, Thorley points out that the use of the media was inordinately expensive and seemed successful only in creating pressure on already severely stretched services.

The deficiencies of the media campaigns in this area stemmed not only from their lack of any clear philosophical direction, but also their irrelevance and inappropriateness to the audience. Often the messages were ill-conceived and displayed a strong southern middle-class media terminology which meant nothing to, or was misunderstood by, the northeastern viewer. A second, more locally based campaign using a celebrity from the area (David Bellamy) as a front man met with wider acclaim and possibly a little success. The aim of the campaign was (a) to give guidelines as to what constitutes 'sensible' drinking and to relate the consequences of overdrinking to the individual's health and social life, and (b) to alert individuals to the fact that alcohol abuse is damaging their community and therefore themselves.

Messages about safe limits were the major thrust of the campaign, with the emphasis on enjoying your drinking encapsulated in the slogan 'Why spoil a good thing?'. Within weeks, the message seemed to have had some effect; Thorley (1985) reported that, for the first time, people were appearing at treatment agencies not with a problem, but simply with concern about their level of consumption. One of the major drawbacks of the campaign, however, was the lack of any follow-up at local level to further the discussion and the impact.

In contrast to the drawbacks of the northeast England media campaigns, the Ministry of Health in France launched a major media campaign in 1978 aimed at reducing the amount of smoking by young people. A campaign was organised at both national and, perhaps more importantly, local level. The main focus of the input by the national media was the showing of three short films at peak viewing times. Coining the slogan 'For every cigarette put out, a little freedom is won', the message aimed to destroy the myths about adult smokers which are often, it is claimed, at the root of the desire to smoke. Television was widely mobilised to put over to young people the message that the various forms of enjoyment they derived from smoking, far from improving their image, were in fact signs of immaturity.

The important difference between this campaign and the previously discussed English attack on drinking, is that the media campaign was only one element of a multifaceted approach. As well as the television coverage, discussions were organised in secondary schools by the Ministry of Education (perhaps one of the advantages of a centrally controlled system!): second, third and fourth-year pupils were brought together on a regular basis to discuss the topic of smoking as a symbol of adulthood.

To follow up the concept of freedom originally introduced by the television coverage, a major national art competition was organised entitled 'To each his chains'. At the same time, regional press conferences made up of teachers and pupils in each region were held to discuss the issues raised by the campaign. Other parts of the campaign included a brochure, *Smoking and Young People* and a teaching package aimed at 9 to 10-year-olds.

Reports by the SOFRES organisation, contained in a study carried out by the Health Education Committee (1980–81) demonstrate that during the time of the campaign, the number of people smoking over the age of 12 fell by 2 000 000. In 1981, only 38.7% of the French people smoked compared with 44.2% in 1976. However, the numbers of young smokers in the 12–18 years age group only decreased by 2% and, as the SOFRES report illustrates, at the conclusion of the campaign, the 16–24 years age group contained more smokers than non-smokers, and young women demonstrated a particular resistance to health messages about smoking.

The conclusions of these media campaigns in two very different areas, and relating to two very different substances, clearly show just how complex the issues are.

Prevention – specific issues

Young people

If preventative interventions specifically orientated towards young people can be devised, then it makes sense to use them rather than attempt to deal with a problem already established in adult life.

In the past, nurses have been involved with young people in schools, often as invited 'experts'. This approach to substance abuse health education, the 'one off' outside speaker usually armed with frightening slides or films, has now generally been rejected in favour of integrating the topic into the overall curriculum. In the development of this approach, it is vital to foster a relationship between the schools and the primary health care nurses, who constitute a source of education for teachers and an important supportive resource.

Working with young people and substance abuse involves the nurses concerned in a close examination of their own values about a different generation. Nowlis (1969 and 1981) identifies a number of important areas to be examined:

1 An understanding of young people and how they learn and develop, their needs and expectations.
2 An understanding of social institutions as organisations and their function for growth and development.
3 A sensitivity to alternative cultures, styles of life and social concepts and mores.
4 Skills in interpersonal communication, problem solving and conflict resolution.

A vital component of any work in the dependency field, particularly when working with somewhat chaotic, emotionally troubled youngsters, is effective teamwork. Due to the involvement of school, family and non-statutory workers in these problems, the nurse in the community may need to reassess the traditionally medical concept of 'team'.

Effective education, self awareness and cohesive teamwork, however, will never stop young people experimenting with mind-altering substances of various kinds. Recognising this limitation means that nurses must address the areas where their input can help reduce the numbers of experimenters (already relatively low) who go on to suffer harm as a result of continued use or misuse.

Harm reduction strategies

Basically, harm reduction techniques can be applied to any area of health education about substance abuse. Even with cigarette smoking, for which the universal message is to stop completely, such techniques can teach the smoker who is not ready to contemplate giving up certain strategies to reduce the risk. For example, smokers can be advised to switch to a low tar brand, put the cigarette out earlier well before reaching the filter, monitor consumption and to cut down if they cannot stop. Similarly, alcohol education has adopted harm reduction approaches by modifying the message from 'thou shalt not' to 'if you do, stick to safe limits'.

Advising young people about the dangers of intoxication, alcoholic poisoning, drinking and driving, and the ways to minimise harm such as 'stick to the same drink' and 'have some food with your drink' all come under harm reduction and form part of the health educational role of nurses. Many health visitors and other specialist community nurses have little trouble accepting harm reduction as a legitimate technique when dealing with legally and socially sanctioned substances, but find the whole discussion much more difficult in relation to solvent abuse or illegal drug use. It is, however, in these two areas particularly that nurses need to grasp the nettle.

Solvents tend to be used by young people in an even more transitory experimental fashion than other substances. Harm reduction techniques, properly utilised, can ensure that the young person lives long enough to grow through the experience. Examining the details of sudden deaths involving solvents, Bass (1970) found that in only 6 cases was a toluene-based glue implicated, whereas 49 sudden deaths were directly caused by aerosols. Another major cause of death, outlined by Brecher (1974), results from using a bag far too big so that, when intoxicated, the user allows it to envelop the face leading to suffocation.

Intoxication results in an exaggerated perception of one's own ability and personal safety. The number of drunken drivers killed and maimed on the roads each year is a sad testimony to that fact. Similarly, solvent abusers facing the social disapproval attached to substance use often choose some isolated, even dangerous, spot to indulge in their habit; canal banks, motorway flyovers, derelict buildings, deserted highrise walkways and flats are all favourite sites for solvent abusers. When the young person is intoxicated or semi-stuporous, these can be dangerous and even fatal locations.

Within an ongoing professional relationship, the therapist's message, 'I would like you to stop using completely, but until that time I am not giving up on you' must be explicit, and the nurse must deliver harm reduction information at each meeting, including the following advice:

1   If you are going to continue to use solvents, then at all costs avoid aerosols.
2   Don't sniff glue from a plastic bag that is big enough to cover your face. Don't do it alone in an isolated place. If you are in a group, make sure someone in the group is not using so much, to keep an eye on the others.

3   Avoid dangerous places such as canal banks, deserted buildings, motorways, etc.
4   Have a clear idea of what you would do if one of your friends collapsed or suffered an accident from using solvents.

Harm or risk reduction techniques are also essential in the health education approach to illegal drug abusers. Often although these individuals remain in contact with services, they are still using drugs. A highly stigmatised and damaged group of patients, they are often seen by health care workers (including nurses) as 'no-hopers', lacking in any motivation to change. The impact of the HIV virus and AIDS has caused health education strategies towards this group to be rethought in fairly revolutionary ways. Injecting drug abusers are the second largest group infected with AIDS outside Africa and have become the most important, in that they form a bridge to two other groups, their sexual partners and their children. Until now, almost all children born infected with HIV virus have had injecting drug abusing parents; similarly, hetero-sexual transmission of the virus in both Europe and the USA has taken place so far mainly via sexual contact with an infected injecting drug abuser. The threat of infection to the wider population is all the more alarming because injecting abusers use prostitution as a common way of funding their habit. In Florida and cities such as New York and San Francisco, 90% of infected prostitutes are or have been injecting drug users.

Initially, health professionals expressed reservations about the possibilities of success with this group. It seemed unlikely that injecting drug users, who continue the habit in full knowledge of the risk to health, and often with personal experience of the resulting physical, emotional and social damage, would change their ways because of something as invisible and untreatable as the AIDS virus. However, although research is still taking place into behaviour patterns amongst this group, the initial impression on both sides of the Atlantic – notably in New York (Des Jarlais *et al.* 1985) and in Britain following the first needle exchange schemes – seems to contradict the stereotype of the injecting drug abuser as incapable of change and unconcerned with health.

Nurses are increasingly involved in long-term risk reduction work with this client group. Techniques include:

1   Providing clear, factual information about infection risk.
2   Offering a 'new for old' sterile needle exchange. Clients are encouraged to come to a centre and exchange old, dirty needles and syringes for new, sterile ones. This not only protects them from the possibility of infection from hepatitis and HIV, but also protects others who may have been put at risk by careless disposal of infected used needles and syringes.

3 This contact gives the nurse the possibility of discussing other factors such as poor technique. Many injecting users turning up at needle exchanges have considerable damage from abscesses, sclerosis of veins and evidence of prolonged use of inappropriate equipment. Faulty techniques, lack of knowledge and adulterated substances can all combine to cause damage to smaller veins, thus forcing users to inject in major ones very early on in their drug-using career. Risk reduction techniques involve nurses in providing instruction on how best to avoid this.

4 Drug abusers who present to an agency operating a needle exchange facility are often in need of broader health care and advice. The ongoing contact and relationship will give the nurse the opportunity to monitor general health, nutrition, and advice on safe sexual practices. Within this non-judgemental relationship, the nurse will also make it clear that the desirable goal is for the individual to move towards a drug-free lifestyle.

All the issues raised by substance abuse are problematic, perhaps none more so than prevention, and it must be said that, in spite of our best efforts, it is the nature of a 'free society' that people have the right to choose to go to hell in their own particular way.

REFERENCES

Bass (1970). Sudden Sniffing Death. *Journal of American Medical Association*, 212, 2075–9.

Brecher E. (1974). *Licit and Illicit Drugs: Consumers Union Report*. Boston: Little Brown & Co.

Davies P. (1985). What is effective prevention. In *The Misuse of Alcohol: Crucial Issues in Dependence, Treatment and Prevention* (Heather N., Robertson I., Davies P. (eds)). Beckenham: Croom Helm.

Des Jarlais D. C., Friedman S. R., Hopkins W. (1985). Risk education for the acquired immuno-deficiency syndrome among intravenous drug users. *Annals of Internal Medicine*, 103, 755–9.

DHSS (1984). *Prevention*. Report of the Advisory Council on the Misuse of Drugs. London: HMSO.

Dorn N., South N. (1987). *A Land Fit for Heroin? Drug Policies, Prevention and Practice*. Basingstoke: Macmillan.

Health Education Committee (1974). *Tyne Tees Alcohol Education Committee – an Evaluation*.

Nowlis H. H. (1969). *Drugs on the College Campus*. New York: Doubleday.

Nowlis H. H. (1981). General issues: prevention is not easy. In *Man, Drugs and Society – Current Perspectives: the proceedings of the 1st Pan Pacific Conference on Drugs and Alcohol, Canberra 1980* (Drew L. R. H., ed). Canberra: AF ADD.

Plant M. A., Deck D. F., Samuel E. (1985). *Alcohol, Drugs and School Leavers*. London: Tavistock.

Stacey B. G. (1981). The use of fear appeals in preventive health education. In *Man, Drugs and Society – Current Perspectives: the proceedings of the 1st Pan Pacific Conference on Drugs and Alcohol, Canberra 1980* (Drew L. R. H., ed). Canberra: AF ADD.

Tether P., Robinson D. (1986). *Preventing Alcohol Problems: A Guide to Local Action*. London: Tavistock.

Thorley A. (1985). The role of mass media campaigns in alcohol health education. In *The Misuse of Alcohol: Crucial Issues in Dependence, Treatment and Prevention* (Heather N., Robertson I., Davies P. (eds)). Beckenham: Croom Helm.

Chapter 8

Models of service provision

In formulating a model service for a particular district, certain issues need to be taken into account and agreed upon. The extent of the problem and the current level of service provision should be assessed; areas of unmet need can be identified, as well as examples of duplication. By basing potential changes in research, it is then possible to build on what already exists to make a more systematic appraisal of impact.

After assessing the extent of the substance problem, a decision has to be made as to the level of resources that should be planned for. Planning can extend to include many groups, as outlined by Ovretveit (1986):

'Planning teams need to concentrate on agreeing and defining general values and philosophy, the mission of the overall service as well as general aims and priorities. Management teams need to concentrate on service objectives and service provision teams are then able to focus on operational objectives.'

The active involvement of current providers of service in this is crucial, and where possible, a consumer's viewpoint should be included.

The commissioning and development of the new service is the next stage in the process. Team building exercises should take place, so that roles and responsibilities can be clarified. Where a multidisciplinary team exists, areas of responsibility to the team and/or manager and one's professional supervisor need to be clarified.

Throughout all this there should be an evaluation of the service. Data on users of the service, including their opinions, and its activity should be collected systematically. Robinson (1986) highlights this problem in an editorial in the *British Journal of Addiction* when commenting upon the information used in a series of recent government reports:

'The basic data they contain to support the policy recommendations they make are rudimentary; overall alcohol consumption and' sales, public drunkenness and drink–driving convictions, alcohol tax revenue, deaths from liver cirrhosis, admissions to hospital and not much else. The data on tobacco are a little better and illicit drugs, understandably, much worse.'

Our aim in this chapter is to provide markers as to how service provisions can be developed and improved. They are meant as examples and do require local interpretation. We also include a critique of the more common approaches to treatment.

ASSESSING THE EXTENT OF THE PROBLEM

Several tools are available for assessing the extent of drug and alcohol problems. Whilst there are commonalities, the assessment process for each substance is described separately.

The drug problem

Hartnoll *et al.* (1985) in their publication *Assessing Local Drug Problems: A Short Guide* provide some guidance for any person wishing to measure the drug problem in their area. Techniques for assessing and monitoring drug problems are described in greater detail in the manual *Drug Problems: Assessing Local Needs*, (which is available from the Drugs Indicator Project (Department of Politics and Sociology, Birkbeck College, 16 Gower Street, London WC1)). These are invaluable resources for any person having the responsibility of assessing the nature and extent of drug misuse. The following sources of information have been outlined in these guides.

Routine statistics
Notifications of narcotic addicts to the Home Office may help, since all doctors are required to notify if they are treating a narcotic addict. However, the forms are not always completed, but when available can be used to indicate trends. Research has suggested that the total prevalence of opioid dependence is probably about five times the notified figure.

Police statistics from the local area include seizures of controlled drugs, and arrests and convictions involving controlled drugs. However, one should note the degree of emphasis placed upon this activity by the local Chief Constable.

Drug-related mortality figures are available from the local coroner, and should include coroner's verdicts of 'death due to drug addiction' and 'death by poisoning'.

Hospital inpatient statistics from both non-psychiatric hospitals (Hospital Activity Analysis) and psychiatric hospitals (Mental Health Enquiry) may also assist. However, a person may be admitted for a drug-related problem and yet be missed out of the statistics. Hepatitis statistics may be useful, as the incidence of type B (serum) hepatitis and of non-A, non-B hepatitis can sometimes be used as an indicator of relatively new cases of drug use by injection. Prescription statistics for psychoactive drugs are of limited value, as they do not outline how the drugs are used or the actual amounts prescribed.

Non-routine information from agencies

Treatment services can provide a useful range of facts, although this will depend upon the style of service. If a drug dependency unit exists, one would expect some systematic data collection including figures on the number of people requesting treatment and those actually engaging in treatment. Details from a sample of general practitioners may help to develop a more accurate local profile. Accident and emergency departments are often in the forefront of treating the acute complications of drug misuse (e.g. overdoses) and figures from them would be useful. Coroners can provide information on deaths of drug users. Probation and aftercare services see many people who misuse drugs and accumulate a considerable amount of information about local problems.

Voluntary agencies, including those who specialise in the treatment of drug users and associated problems, e.g. homelessness and legal problems, can also assist. These agencies usually collect some basic data (e.g. age, sex, definition of drug problem, intervention made by agency) which can complement that available from specialists.

Social services see many people with drug problems and may be able to provide some figures. However, the cases are not always obvious in this area, and therefore it may be appropriate to select a particular time scale for intensive investigations.

Information from drug users and others in the community

These sources are often neglected by researchers and yet form a vital component of any assessment. Drug takers can provide a first-hand account of the position, including perception of local treatment agencies and police activity. Self-help groups are often in touch with people who are not attending agencies, as are community or tenants' associations.

The people and agencies outlined above will provide information helpful in determining the extent of the drug problem. However, any workers receiving this information should provide continuous feedback in return, since the process of information exchange is vital. Whilst assessing the extent of the problem, researchers should be developing an awareness of the way that services liaise and cooperate.

The alcohol problem

Many of the sources used in evaluating the extent of the drug problem can help in assessing the size of the alcohol problem. Useful information includes alcohol-related mortality figures (hospital and coroners'), hospital inpatient statistics (non-psychiatric and psychiatric), information from treatment services, accident and emergency departments, police, probation service, voluntary agencies, social services and self-help groups. In addition, local population profiles can be tentatively correlated with national findings. For example, there is considerable evidence about excessive drinking in the 18–24 age group (13% of men and 4% of women exceed the accepted safe limits) and a local focus from the national figures may help to refine the picture. However, many thousands of people experiencing various alcohol-related problems are not recognised or detected by the services outlined above.

Edwards *et al.* (1972) looked at the drinking habits in a London suburb in 1965. The results indicated that 7% of men and 10% of women were abstainers, 17% and 36% respectively were occasional drinkers, 9% and 20% were light drinkers, 25% and 28% were frequent light drinkers, 26% and 6% moderate drinkers and 14% of men and no women were heavy drinkers. Edwards *et al.* concluded that there is no single drinking pattern, but there are patterns amongst different social classes and sexes that might be labelled either 'problem drinking' or 'alcoholism' depending upon the environment and level of support available.

The importance of gaining a comprehensive picture was highlighted by Cartwright *et al.* (1975) when they compared the number of people with drinking problems in an English health district with the number of people treated. This district had an alcohol treatment unit as well as Alcoholics Anonymous and Al-Anon groups, a local council on alcoholism and a hostel. Of a sample of 286 local residents, 0.7% felt they had current problems with alcohol and 2.4% reported having had problems in the past. During the same year as the general population study, only 0.16% of the adult population of the district were treated for alcoholism by a psychiatric service of any kind in the area.

Optimal use should be made of other sources to make the assessment as accurate as possible. Are there any large district general hospitals (where a number of the patients may be abnormal drinkers) and 'high risk' industries (large breweries or distilleries) in the area? These local influences can play an important part in fine-tuning the service provided to cope with the extent of the problem.

Solvent misuse

Hard evidence about the extent of solvent misuse is not easy to find. It is unlikely that treatment services will have contact with many solvent misusers. Some useful sources of subjective data include schools (school nurses and teachers), youth counselling services, youth leaders and community or tenants' associations. The police are unlikely to have accurate figures, as arrests of solvent misusers are rare: children found sniffing glue are usually taken home.

Having completed the formal procedure of assessing the extent of the substance abuse problem, it should then be presented in a style that provides opportunity for discussion of proposed developments. A particularly good example of this is *Drug, Alcohol and Solvent Misuse in Waltham Forest* by Robert Crusz (1986).

PLANNING THE SERVICE

Ovretveit (1986) has outlined the different levels of planning that need to take place. Initially there needs to be agreement at district health authority level about the general philosophy of the proposed service, as well as the setting of priorities and an associated time scale. Effective joint planning in both health and social services is necessary, and should also involve the voluntary organisations. This view is highlighted by the reports of the Advisory Council on the Misuse of Drugs (DHSS 1982) and the Advisory Committee on Alcoholism (DHSS 1978). Membership of the planning team, as well as including health and social services planners and administrators, should include clinical representatives (Fig.8.1). A definite commitment to the role of voluntary organisations must be identified by the provision of membership places to such organisations.

Developing and improving the service

It would be extremely rare to be developing a new service in a vacuum. Although there might not be a specialist health or social services facility, self-help groups may already have mushroomed. Similarly, some local authority voluntary groups (often partially funded by the health and local authority) may exist. There may be a physician who has a particular interest in working with problem drinkers, or a liver unit which encounters any substance misusers. Clear lines of communication should exist between all those clinically involved to ensure that duplication does not happen.

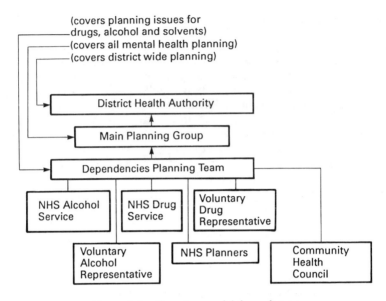

(covers planning issues for drugs, alcohol and solvents)
(covers all mental health planning)
(covers district wide planning)

District Health Authority

Main Planning Group

Dependencies Planning Team

NHS Alcohol Service

NHS Drug Service

Voluntary Drug Representative

Voluntary Alcohol Representative

NHS Planners

Community Health Council

Figure 8.1   *Planning model for a district*
Note: This is a hypothetical example; not all of the local services shown would necessarily be represented in each area. Some areas might have a rehabilitation hostel but no community treatment unit, whilst the reverse might be true in other areas.

Liaison groups
Liaison communication between agencies needs to be more than a telephone or paper exercise. A regular meeting between the services should be arranged, dealing with mutual clients, identification of unmet needs, briefing of planners and coordination of joint clinical activities. Without regular meetings the possibility of mutual distrust is great, especially since several services may be after the same funds. Our experience shows that joint client and clinical work is a valuable way of improving liaison and cooperation. For example, within the Camden, Bloomsbury and Islington areas, a video has just been produced for teaching purposes by a liaison group of statutory and non-statutory agencies including social services (Arlington House), the Alcohol Problem Advisory Service, Alcohol Recovery Project, CASA Alcohol Services, the Women's Alcohol Centre and the Rugby House Project. This group was formed to offer a support network of various treatment options, as each individual agency was very aware of the problems of becoming isolated. The video is entitled 'A Coordinated Alcohol Service' and is available by contacting the Alcohol Advisory Service. It describes not only the individual agencies, but also how each agency can draw on resources offered by the group as a whole.

Joint dependency services

This is a matter of considerable debate. Should services for people with drug and alcohol problems amalgamate, cooperate or remain separate? There is no easy answer. There are examples nationally of areas where joint dependency services work well (Newcastle), and areas where separate services work well (Bloomsbury). There is growing evidence that some clients do cross over in their use of substances, and this needs to be acknowledged by local services. There are, however, major differences (in respect of age, sex, problem duration and accommodation status) between clients who use drug services and those using alcohol services.

We advise two notes of caution when considering joint dependency services. Firstly, is it something that the clients have been consulted upon? Secondly, joint dependency services can sometimes be a smokescreen for providing one or both services on the cheap. You should be confident that both these areas have been checked out before proceeding.

Model of local services

Fig.8.2 is an extract from a paper entitled *Strategies for Services for Problem Drinkers in Greater London*, produced by the London Boroughs working party on drug and alcohol problems in January 1986.

Whilst the focus of this model is the provision of services for problem drinkers, it is also relevant to problem drug users. The Advisory Committee on Alcohol believes that 'every person with a drinking problem should be able to find the help he or she needs'. This view is endorsed by the Advisory Council on the Misuse of Drugs. There is no single approach or professional group that has a right or responsibility to treat substance misusers; however, the following elements are required in a local service:

1   Advice and information centres to act as a focal point for services in the area and make referrals to other agencies.
2   Counselling services which are available for the clients, their families and colleagues.
3   Self-help groups – these should be provided with active support, e.g. provision of rooms.
4   Detoxification facilities, which need to be easily available; access to beds in a medical or psychiatric setting is probably a more realistic option than a specialist detoxification unit.
5   Other services, possibly covering a larger catchment area, e.g. rehabilitation hostels, women's centres and inpatient hospital units. These also include services for ethnic minorities, lesbians and gay men, and persistent offenders.

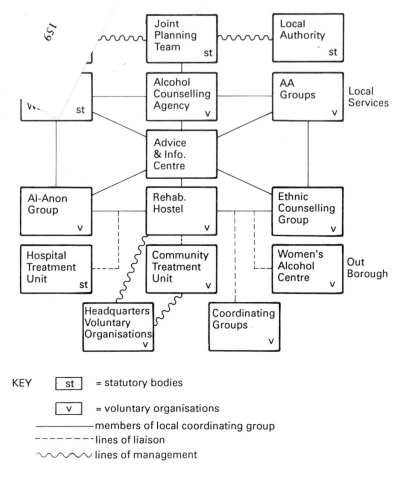

Figure 8.2   *Model for local alcohol services*

SERVICE EVALUATION

Having built up a clear picture of the extent of the substance problem in an area and subsequently developed or improved the coordination of services, systematic collection of data should continue. This should include an annual updating of the figures from the sources outlined previously; in addition, there should be systematic data collection on all clients in contact with the services. Data should include the following: sex, age, marital status (single, married/cohabiting, widowed, separated/divorced), employment status (fulltime, part-time, unemployed, retired, school/student, houseperson), income (private, earnings, state benefit, pension, dependent, maintenance, no income), accommodation (owner occupier, rented, hostel, bed and breakfast, squatting, no fixed abode), referring sources (will be locally determined), family structure (lives alone, lives with friend, lives with spouse/cohabitee, lives with spouse and children, lives alone with children, lives with parents) and main intervention following assessment (locally determined). Information about problem duration and amounts and type of drugs or alcohol consumed should also be recorded.

Follow-up work on clients is often seen as an area of great difficulty. Treatment services, attempting to define success or failure rates, report major difficulties in developing adequate evaluation procedures. There are many reasons for this, including a high level of client drop-out and attrition, and resistance by clinical workers. Whilst there are serious ethical dilemmas about research on 'treatment' and 'no treatment' groups, this dimension rarely becomes an issue since few services follow up clients in the first place! Follow-up needs to be locally determined and matched with the treatment philosophy of the service. If an agency is totally abstinence orientated, then clients who have returned to trouble-free substance use will either not attend or will be deemed as failures. Experience in the Alcohol Problem Advisory Service highlights these difficulties. This has meant for the service, a redefinition of evaluation and to now regard the process of evaluation as an ongoing assessment on the individual's treatment programme which takes into account the client's subjective views of the treatment received and that a well-integrated follow-up system can evolve into an aftercare facility which embraces the concept of continuity of care.

COMMON APPROACHES TO TREATMENT

A useful starting point for any review of treatment approaches is a statement by Jonathan Chick (1984):

> 'Many professionals, including doctors, hold a pessimistic view of alcoholism. They see alcoholics as sliding downhill, perhaps with brief plateaux, with few if any recovering. However, this stereotype may be based on only a small number of clients who keep on and on relapsing.'

When working with problem drug-takers or drinkers, it is often worth remembering (for the sake of one's own morale if nothing else) that many of the clients we see are those with serious problems, and those who return are clients who continue to have problems or relapse.

Because of the general attitudes to substance use and the acknowledgement of such a problem, many clients who recover will want to put that
period behind them, and are unlikely to call the nurse to say that all is
well.

We review here the approaches made by three main groups: the
National Health Service, voluntary organisations and self-help groups.

The National Health Service

Services for drug takers

The report of the Brain Committee recommended that the right to
maintain addicts on heroin be restricted to a limited number of doctors,
and that centres should be set up to which addicts could go for
treatment when their usual doctors could no longer prescribe. In 1968,
14 such centres were set up in London and 11 in the provinces. These
became known as drug dependency units (DDUs), and remained for
many years the typical NHS response to problem drug takers. The
clinics usually have a very strict regimen of prescribing and clients are
expected to attend a specific number of times. In addition to
prescribing, the clinics provide support either individually or in a group
setting. A remarkable feature of some DDUs is that they will only treat
people with an opiate problem, and a client attending with a
tranquilliser difficulty may not be treated. There is little uniformity in
respect of activity, e.g. prescribing policies, staff numbers and opening
times. Most DDUs have a catchment area of several district health
authorities, and this limits the amount of access of clients.

The middle of the 1980s saw an increase in the services provided to
drug users by the NHS. Community drug teams, often funded by
central government monies for a three-year period, have developed in
several areas. The teams usually consist of a coordinator, social
worker, community psychiatric nurse, health education and training
officer, secretary and part-time medical staff. These developments have
been somewhat sporadic and are often dependent on local initiative
and enthusiasm. Such a model has been endorsed by the Advisory
Council on the Misuse of Drugs, which has recommended that regional
drug problem teams should also be set up and should have 'a peri-
patetic role within the region giving support and advice to, and liaising
with, specialist and non-specialist agencies and encouraging the development of new services'. It is still early days for the community drug teams,
but it is obvious that they face the same problems as the community
alcohol teams in balancing the demands of direct clinical work, health
education and consultancy to non-specialist workers. They have the
advantage of being able to focus their work in a specific catchment area,
usually of a smaller size than the DDUs. The crunch for some of those will
come when central monies no longer exist and local districts are asked

to refund. The development of the Drug Advisory Service (under the auspices of the Health Advisory Service) provides opportunities for monitoring services in an interactive and dynamic way.

Services for problem drinkers
In the late 1950s the first specialised NHS alcohol treatment unit (ATU) was established, and to date nearly thirty have been put into operation. Ettore (1984) completed a major study of ATUs between December 1978 and March 1982. She concluded that there was no stereotypical unit and found a great diversity in treatment objectives (whether or not units required total abstinence or used a controlled drinking regimen), treatment procedures and treatment philosophies. There was evidence that the ATUs provided highly specialised treatment for a highly select group of patients. Generally, the units provided a period of inpatient care, usually preceded by detoxification. The average length of stay in 1987 was six weeks, with a major focus on group-based activity. ATUs give problem drinkers a useful opportunity to reflect on their situation, but although clients may learn to deal with their problems while in the unit, they may run into difficulties when discharged. In many cases, the units have a regional health authority catchment area, which can cause serious problems for clients in relation to transport, maintenance of family contact and ongoing support. The majority of ATUs are in the grounds of large psychiatric institutions, and thus to the stigma of having an alcohol problem is added that of having a mental disorder.

During the 1970s, departmental policy in England and Wales changed from the goal of highly specialised psychiatric services to the goal of an integrated community service. It was suggested by the DHSS that the ATU might become 'a local focus of expertise, training and research'. Community alcohol teams (CATs) began to develop, and there are less than ten operating in the UK. Their role is usually a combination of the following:

1 Undertaking education and training.
2 Providing consultancy to health and social services workers in the field who need advice and support.
3 Undertaking a limited amount of clinical work.

The teams vary greatly in size, most having a fulltime nurse or social worker with sessional input from other professionals. More realistic-ally staffed CATs have been developed in Leicestershire and in Bloomsbury, where there are several fulltime workers in the service. To expect one person to have an impact either clinically or educationally is totally unrealistic, whereas a larger team with the resources to provide a locally based, multivariate approach is more sensible. Health circular [HN(89)4] is helpful in providing advice about the ways organisations can work more effectively together.

Services for solvent misusers

The development of services for solvent misusers has been even more sporadic, except for the occasional professional taking a special interest and thereby gaining the skills to work with these clients. The other exception to this is work completed in Glasgow and the Solvent Abuse Helpline in south London.

Voluntary organisations

There is a great range of organisations providing treatment for problem drug takers and drinkers. These organisations are sometimes referred to as the 'non-statutory sector', referring to the fact that they have no legal accountability to the Health Service for their work. Many of these services have developed a joint approach to 'addictive problems', and rather than describe their philosophies by substance, we have categorised them as community or residential projects.

Community projects

The main lead in this area was taken by the Local Councils on Alcoholism who were allied to the National Council on Alcoholism before it was disbanded in 1983. Since then, some councils have continued to concentrate on problem drinkers, but others have developed a response to problem drug takers. Most councils have a fulltime director or coordinator; beyond that, their level of staffing depends upon finance and local commitment. Some have paid employees (e.g. the Greater London Alcohol Advisory Service), whilst others rely on the energies of volunteer counsellors (e.g. the Essex Alcohol Advisory Service). Most of their activity is the provision of regular counselling, although a few projects have developed a more intensive programme: specific examples are the Lifeline project in Manchester and ACCEPT in London. A distinct advantage that voluntary organisations have over the NHS is their limited bureaucracy. In addition to the director, there is usually a management committee, and it is usually at this level that decisions can be reached. It means that they can often respond quickly to changes in demand by clients. Unfortunately their funding is often precarious, and much of the energies of the director is directed towards maintaining financial solvency. The range of funders often include central government, local boroughs or health authorities and donations from clients. However, partial funding from one source is often dependent upon funding from another, and thus the game of financial 'table tennis' is perpetuated.

Residential projects

For many substance users, especially those who have developed particularly serious problems, a period of residential rehabilitation is required so that they can gain the skills to deal with their drug or alcohol problem and its associated complications. The majority of rehabilitation houses are abstinence orientated, although there are still some projects that focus primarily on a particular substance, e.g. the Alcohol Recovery Project. Other organisations such as Turning Point and Aquarius have facilities that are aimed at particular substances (e.g. opiates or alcohol), but within the organisation clients can move on to other facilities should their drug of use change. The general principle of residential rehabilitation is to provide clients with an initial period of intensive support, and over a period of time to increase the amount of responsibility and independence they are given. Group work forms the basis of much of the work, as does life and social skills training.

Self-help groups

The development of self-help groups has been spearheaded by Alcoholics Anonymous (AA). In May 1935, Bill Wilson and Dr Bob met and talked about their problems in gaining sobriety and began to look for others in a similar state. By 1939 the membership had increased to about a hundred, and a book of members' stories was published under the title *Alcoholics Anonymous*. It now claims over one million members in over a hundred countries. AA's programme of recovery is contained in the 'Twelve Steps':

1 We admitted we were powerless over alcohol – that our lives had become unmanageable.
2 Came to believe that a power greater than ourselves could restore us to sanity.
3 Made a decision to turn our will and our lives over to the care of God as we understood Him.
4 Made a searching and fearless moral inventory of ourselves.
5 Admitted to God, to ourselves and to another human being the exact nature of our wrongs.
6 We are entirely ready to have God remove all these defects of character.
7 Humbly asked Him to remove our shortcomings.
8 Made a list of all persons we had harmed and became willing to make amends to them all.
9 Made direct amends to such people wherever possible, except when to do so would injure them or others.
10 Continued to take personal inventory, and when we were wrong, promptly admitted it.
11 Sought through prayer and meditation to improve our conscious contact with God as we understood Him, praying only for knowledge of His will for us and the power to carry that out.

12   Having had a spiritual awakening as the result of these steps, we tried to carry this message to alcoholics and to practise these principles in our affairs.

Whilst there are religious connotations to the Twelve Steps, AA would argue that religious denomination is not an issue. For many problem drinkers AA is a lifeline and has become the key to their return to a successful abstinence-orientated life. The content and style of groups even in a small locality can vary, being dependent upon the membership. When advising people to attend AA, it is useful to ask them to attend several meetings in different areas, as they may find one particular group and its members more attractive than others. Meetings are held at all times of the day and night, with approximately 200 in London on an average week. Open meetings are also held, which are open to the members of the general public, and attending one is one of the most useful ways of finding out about the work of AA.

Al–Anon is a self-help group for the spouses, relatives and friends of problem drinkers. The group is particularly valuable in providing support.

Al-Ateen is a self-help group for the children of problem drinkers. The contact for this group is Al-Anon.

Narcotics Anonymous (NA) has been growing at a rapid rate since the late 1970s. It has taken on a similar model as Alcoholics Anonymous acting as a fellowship for people with drug problems.

Ad-Fam has been set up to give support to the families of drug users.

There are a few less well-known self-help groups, which are gradually developing a network. Drinkwatchers has been set up to aim a message of sensible drinking at the general public and has a strong behavioural basis to its work. Tranx is a self-help group for people wishing to deal with their dependence on tranquillisers.

Conclusion

This chapter summarises the more common approaches to treatment. No single mode has proved to be any more successful than the next. Treatment programmes and interventions should be tailored to the specific needs of the individual client, and the *modus operandi* (e.g. waiting time, environment, etc.) should be of a standard that we would find acceptable ourselves, were we in the client's position.

REFERENCES

Cartwright A. K. J., Shaw S. J., Sprately T. A. (1975). *Designing a Comprehensive Community Response to Problems of Alcohol Abuse.* Report to the DHSS by the Maudsley Alcohol Pilot Project. London: HMSO.

Chick J. (1984). *Drinking Problems – Patterns of Recovery and the Effect of Treatment*. Occasional Paper no.3. London: Institute of Alcohol Studies.

Crusz R. (1986). *Drug, Alcohol and Solvent Misuse in Waltham Forest*. Woodford Bridge, Essex: Waltham Forest Health Authority, Claybury Hospital.

DHSS (1978). *The Pattern and Range of Services for Problem Drinkers*. Report of the Advisory Committee on Alcoholism. London: HMSO.

DHSS (1982). *Treatment and Rehabilitations*. Report of the Advisory Council on the Misuse of Drugs. London: HMSO.

Edwards G., Chandler J., Hensman C. (1972). Drinking in a London suburb. *Quarterly Journal for The Study of Alcohol*, Suppl. 6, 69–93.

Ettore E. M. (1984). *A Study of Alcoholism Treatment Units: Treatment Activities and the Institutional Response*, Unpublished Paper, London: Addiction Research Unit.

Hartnoll R., Mitcheson M., Lewis R., Daviaud E. (1985). *Assessing Local Drug Problems: A Short Guide*. London: Drug Indicators Project.

Ovretveit J. (1986). *Organisation of Multidisciplinary Community Teams*, Brunel Institute of Organisation and Social Studies.

Robinson D. (1986). Basic data for informed debate. *British Journal of Addiction*, **81**, 6.

Chapter 9

The need for research, evaluation and education

RESEARCH AND EVALUATION – THE WAY FORWARD

Until quite recently, it has unfortunately been very rare for nurses working in the field of substance misuse to be involved in research, even at a fairly basic level. The pressures of extensive clinical commitments, combined with limited resources and difficulty in getting access to any formal training or education, have resulted in a lack of confidence in this area.

In the last five years, however, the field has undergone a welcome and significant change which, although still relatively small, is nevertheless having a fundamental impact on substance abuse nursing. This new departure stems mainly from the inclusion of research methods into the curriculum of many specialist and generic nursing courses, and this newly acquired confidence and expertise of nurses in research techniques is producing important insights into many areas of nursing intervention and service delivery.

There is now a growing expectation that clinical nurses, nurse educators and managers will be able to undertake small-scale research projects in order to evaluate their work. Similarly, nurse specialists are increasingly expected to have the ability to critically appraise and use the results of research reports in their practice.

In the present period of rapid change in substance abuse nursing, research will be a vital factor if the profession is to evaluate efficiently the care and service offered to clients, their families and the community. However, if these currently encouraging trends are to be developed further, the most crucial element will be the provision of appropriate professional education.

FRAMEWORK FOR NURSING EDUCATION

Leaving aside the hysteria displayed in relation to drugs by the tabloid press, it remains the case that since the early 1980s Britain (along with most of Europe and the USA) has seen a large increase in the availability and use of illegal drugs. Similar increases have taken place in the same period with legal drugs, such as alcohol, tranquillisers and 'over the counter' drugs. Whilst pointing out that Britain has moved from a situation in which heroin dependence was rare, to one in which an increasingly worrying number of young people smoke or inject heroin, the Royal College of Psychiatrists (1987) also point out that in 1985 over 39 million prescriptions were dispensed for tranquillisers alone. Large numbers of so-called 'innocent addicts' are now being championed by the media in legal battles with doctors over such prescribing practices.

Illegal drug use must be placed in perspective, and nursing needs to enter into an informed debate in relation to all levels of substance misuse among clients. The move away from the orthodoxy of abstinence for those in difficulties with alcohol or drugs means that nursing requires a new framework for the consideration of causal factors.

One such framework is the interaction model of dependency nursing utilised on the specialist course ENB 612 at Manchester Polytechnic (Fig. 9.1). By viewing dependence on drugs or alcohol as a changing, dynamic process influenced by a myriad factors both within the individual and from the social environment, nurses are better able to tailor assessment, intervention and evaluation to the individual client's needs.

Similarly, it is possible to extend the framework to describe the subject areas that are required to inform a curriculum aimed at specialist nurses (Fig. 9.2).

This model of nursing allows flexibility of response based on informed therapeutic choices at various points in the client's problem drug-taking or drinking career.

The issues presented by clients with drug and alcohol problems are many and varied, and change for better or worse at various stages in their lives. Nursing must be able to respond effectively with a selection of therapeutic, educational or supportive choices that make sense to the client. In order to achieve this we require a strategy to improve training in drug and alcohol issues for all nurses.

Basic level training

Nurses undertaking basic nurse training for all parts of the register should be taught to recognise alcohol and drug problems at an early stage in their development. Early detection of problems by nurses can be invaluable in helping the client before too much damage is done, thereby saving much misery for the client and scarce resources for the community.

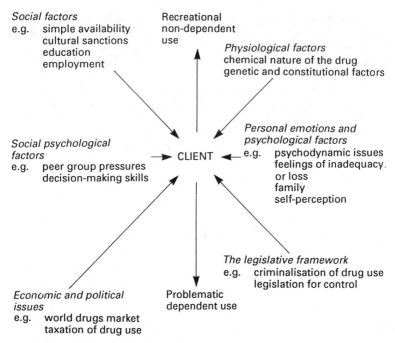

Social factors
e.g. simple availability
      cultural sanctions
      education
      employment

Recreational
non-dependent
use

Physiological factors
chemical nature of the drug
genetic and constitutional factors

*Social psychological
factors*
e.g. peer group pressures
      decision-making skills

→ CLIENT ←

*Personal emotions and
psychological factors*
e.g. psychodynamic issues
      feelings of inadequacy,
      or loss
      family
      self-perception

The legislative framework
e.g. criminalisation of drug use
      legislation for control

*Economic and political
issues*
e.g. world drugs market
      taxation of drug use

Problematic
dependent use

This multidimensional view of the forces acting to produce drug
use or misuse can be utilised to plan the theoretical base needed
to inform nurses working with this often difficult client group.

Figure 9.1 *Forces acting upon the individual*

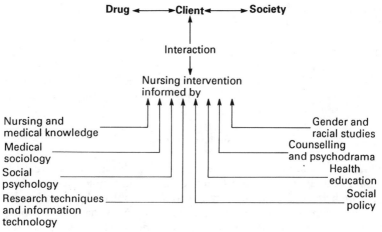

Drug ←——→ Client ←——→ Society

Interaction

Nursing intervention
informed by

Nursing and
medical knowledge

Medical
sociology

Social
psychology

Research techniques
and information
technology

Gender and
racial studies

Counselling
and psychodrama

Health
education

Social
policy

Figure 9.2 *Continuum of informed therapeutic choice*

This increased training at basic level would create trained nurses who would always be aware of the possibility that the presenting physical or psychological problem of the patient is in fact masking an underlying problem of dependency on drugs or alcohol.

Primary care nurses

Increasing numbers of trained nurses now work in the community and consequently meet many clients for whom the major issue is problem drug taking or drinking. Simply being able to recognise the problem is not enough for this group of practitioners: further training on initial assessment and basic intervention strategies for less complex cases is required. Additionally, nurses working with individuals and families in the community need to be made more aware of lines of communication for help and referral. Short training courses such as those developed by the English National Board for Nursing Midwifery and Health Visiting would undoubtedly fill this major gap in training and provision.

Specialist nurses

Since the report by the Advisory Council on the Misuse of Drugs, *Training and Rehabilitation* (DHSS 1982), five courses were set up in Britain for training specialist nurses in this field. Nurses are the largest group of professionals working as specialists in the statutory drug and alcohol sector. These courses have been very important in breaking new ground for nursing, producing nurses who are not only well versed in all aspects of the problem, but are also skilled in intervention, education and research. These specialists operate as treatment agents within both community and inpatient settings, and most importantly also serve as essential advice and back-up to other workers, particularly primary care nurses.

Nursing is an essential resource in helping individuals, families and society deal with drug and alcohol problems. By demonstrating that dependent clients are not a hopeless prognostic case, nurses can demolish many of the negative myths surrounding such work.

The way forward for nursing is to develop our strategy of training nurses in this field and, by doing so, to assist many more clients to overcome the destructive influences of drug and alcohol dependency.

REFERENCES

DHSS (1982). *Training and Rehabilitation.* Report of the Advisory Council on the Misuse of Drugs. London: HMSO.
Royal College of Psychiatrists (1987). *Drug Scenes. A Report on Drugs and Drug Dependence.* Gaskell.

Select bibliography

Alcoholics Anonymous. (1976). *The Big Book*. London: AA Sterling Area Services.

Edward G. (1982). *The Treatment of Drinking Problems*. Oxford: Blackwell.

Gossop M. (1982). *Living with Drugs*. London: Temple Smith.

Jamieson A., Glanz A., MacGregor S. (1984). *Dealing with Drug Misuse – Crisis Intervention in the City*. London: Tavistock Publications.

Miller W. R. (1980). *The Addictive Behaviours, Treatment of Alcoholism, Drug Abuse, Smoking and Obesity*. Oxford: Pergamon Press.

Plant M. A. (1982). *Drinking and Problem Drinking*. London: Junction Books.

Royal College of General Practitioners (1986). *Alcohol – A Balanced View*.

Royal College of Psychiatrists (1986). *Alcohol – Our Favourite Drug*. London: Tavistock Publications.

Shaw S., Cartwright A., Spratley T., Harwin J. (1978). *Responding to Drinking Problems*. London: Croom Helm.

Social Services Committee (1985). *Misuse of Drugs*. London: HMSO.

Useful addresses

Ad–Fam National Office
Unit 7
South Thames Studios
5–11 Lavington Street
London SE1 0NZ
Tel: 01 401 2079

Works with the families of drug users, setting up family support groups around the country and education and prevention. Run their own training courses. Campaign for wider range of treatments and services for families and drug users.

Al-Anon
61 Great Dover Street
London SE1 4YF
Tel: 01 403 0888

An organisation for the relatives and friends of people with a drink problem.

Alcohol Concern
305 Gray's Inn Road
London WC1X 8QF
Tel: 01 833 3471

Alcohol Concern's objectives are to improve the services available to problem drinkers, promote a better public understanding of the problem, and to reduce the incidence of alcohol abuse.

Alcoholics Anonymous
PO Box 1
Stonebow House
Stonebow
York YO1 2UJ
Tel: 0904 644026

Self-help organisation run on the lines of group therapy.

Drugs Indicator Project
Department of Politics and Sociology
Birkbeck College
16 Gower Street
London WC1

Drugs Training Project
Department of Sociology
University of Stirling
Stirling FK9 4LE
Tel: 0786 73171 (extensions 1774/1775)

Agency offering training and education to drug workers throughout Scotland.

Families Anonymous
Rooms 20/21
c/o Community Services
567 Parsons Lane
London SW6 4HP
Tel: 01 224 1229

Self-help group for families and friends of people with drink problems.

Greater London Alcohol Advisory Service (GLASS)
91 Charterhouse Street
London EC1M 6HR
Tel: 01 253 6221

An advice and information service for the London area.

Health Education Authority
Hamilton House
Mableton Place
London WC1H 9TX
Tel: 01 631 0930

Institute for the Study of Drug Dependence
1–4 Hatton Place
Hatton Garden
London EC1N 8ND
Tel: 01 430 1991

A library and information service on all aspects of problem drug use.

Institute of Alcohol Studies
Alliance House
Caxton Street
London SW1H 0RS
Tel: 01 222 5880

An educational charity which provides information, publishes papers, organises conferences and workshops and initiates research on alcohol use and abuse.

London Lighthouse
111–117 Lancaster Road
London W11 1QT
Tel: 01 792 1200

Residential and counselling centre for people affected by HIV and AIDS.

Narcotics Anonymous
PO Box 417
London SW10 0DP

A self-help fellowship of men and women for whom drugs have become a major problem, the *only* requirement for membership being a desire to stop using.

National Campaign Against Solvent Abuse
The Enterprise Centre
444 Brixton Road
London SW9 8EJ
Tel: 01 733 7330

The only national charity dealing purely with solvent abuse, offering counselling, support and information.

Nurses Welfare Service
Victoria Chambers
16–18 Strutton Ground
London SW1P 2HP
Tel: 01 222 1563

Consultation for members of the profession who have been referred to the governing bodies with their right of fitness to practice in question.

Release
169 Commercial Street
London E1 6BW
Tel: 01 377 5905
    24-hour helpline 01 603 8654 (operator referral)

Independent national agency concerned with the welfare of people using drugs.

Scottish Drug Forum
266 Clyde Street
Glasgow G1 4JH
Tel: 041 221 1175

Scottish equivalent of SCODA (see below).

South Wales Association for Prevention of Addiction (SWAPA)
1 Neville Street
Cardiff CF1 8LP
Tel: 0222 383313

All Wales drugline telephone counselling service for anyone who needs advice on drug problems.

Standing Conference on Drug Abuse (SCODA)
1–4 Hatton Place
Hatton Garden
London EC1N 8ND
Tel: 01 430 2341

National organisation providing information and advice on the availability of local or regional specialist drugs services.

TACADE (Training Consultancy Resources in Health, Personal, Social and Drug Education)
3rd Floor
Furness House
Trafford Road
Salford M5 2XJ
Tel: 061 848 0351

TACADE is the only organisation of its kind in the UK. There are three major strands to its work; the production of resources; the provision of training courses for a range of professional groups who are involved in health and drug education; the provision of advice, information, support and consultancy to any individual, group or organisation requiring help concerning the issue of health or drugs.

Terence Higgins Trust
BM Aids
London WC1N 3XX
Tel: 01 831 0330

Telephone line service providing advice and assistance to people requiring further information about HIV.

Triple A (Action on Alcohol Abuse)
3rd Floor
Livingstone House
11 Carteret Street
London SW1H 9DL
Tel: 01 222 3454

National campaign for safe and sensible drinking.

Index